Lewis Este Mills

Glimpses of Southern France and Spain

Lewis Este Mills

Glimpses of Southern France and Spain

ISBN/EAN: 9783337245207

Printed in Europe, USA, Canada, Australia, Japan

Cover: Foto ©ninafisch / pixelio.de

More available books at **www.hansebooks.com**

Glimpses

OF

Southern France

AND

Spain.

L. E. MILLS.

CINCINNATI:
ROBERT CLARKE & CO. PUBLISHERS, 65 WEST FOURTH ST.
1867.

Southern France and Spain.

Contents.

CHAPTER I.
Lyons . 1

CHAPTER II.
Avignon . . . 14

CHAPTER III.
Nismes—Pont du Gard 21

CHAPTER IV.
Toulouse—Bordeaux—Pau—Bayonne . 29

CHAPTER V.
Irun—Burgos 37

CHAPTER VI.
Valladolid—Escorial . 49

CHAPTER VII.
Madrid . . . 55

CHAPTER VIII.
Toledo—La Mancha 70

CONTENTS.—Continued.

CHAPTER IX.
Cordova   81

CHAPTER X.
Seville   86

CHAPTER XI.
Cadiz—Gibraltar   99

CHAPTER XII.
Malaga   112

CHAPTER XIII.
Granada—Madrid—Saragofsa—Barcelona   120

CHAPTER XIV.
Leaving Spain   131

CHAPTER XV.
General Remarks   139

Preface.

This little book, composed during my leisure hours, is mainly transcribed from letters and a journal written during a short trip through Southern France and Spain.

I can only hope that its readers will find as much amusement in the perusal, as I have found in the writing of it.

Cincinnati, March, 1867.

Chapter I.—*Lyons.*

ON the 25th of January, 1865, we left Paris by rail, for Lyons. The distance is 316 miles, which we traversed in about 11 hours. And just here, at the beginning of our travel, I wish to record my opinion—founded upon considerable experience—that the commonly accepted theory that second-claſs cars upon the Continent are as good as the first, as well as much cheaper, is a delusion and a snare. They are cheaper, but are neither so luxurious, so comfortable, nor so clean; while they generally contain a claſs of people who are not so agreeable to meet as those traveling in the first-claſs cars. Of course, if one is under the necefsity of studying economy in traveling, he must take second-clafs cars instead of first, and small rooms in retired quarters, in the place of apartments more commodious and convenient, and dine at plain restaurants instead of at the best, and be content therewith, like a sensible man; but he should not attempt to make every one else believe that he would not have something better if he could afford it.

The cars are luxurious coaches; the *buffets*, or eating houses, on the route, unlike those in America, are clean and attractive—provided with snow-white table-cloths and napkins, good food, table wine, first rate coffee, attentive waiters, and withal, reasonable charges. Ample time is allowed for meals, and every five minutes is sounded through the room the voice of a waiter, crying out the number of minutes that remain before the starting of the train, so that no one is hurried. Hot water footstools are in each car, warming the feet, and leaving the head cool, and there are no cries of boys, passing through the cars with "pies, pies, pies," "lozenges, two cents a roll,"

Chapter I.—Lyons.

"figs, pop-corn and jujube paste," and similar provocations to dyspepsia. Guards are ready, in uniform, at every station, to answer questions; there is no hurry or confusion, and thus the disagreeableneſs of traveling is mitigated as far as poſsible.

The country through which we paſsed is fertile, and filled with gardens, and the trees are trimmed, as is the custom in France, so as to yield the greatest amount of small branches for firewood. The hills paſsed in traversing Burgundy are literally vine-clad. The railroad, like those in England, is built with great care and expense, with bridges as carefully finished as if the stonework were for a dwelling house, and with embankments either sodded or walled with stone.

About ten o'clock in the evening we arrived, and went to the *Hotel de l'Europe*, where, on the second floor, we secured rooms both comfortable and of moderate price. The town is the second in France in point of population and wealth. It stands on both banks of the Saône and the Rhone, but the larger part occupies the tongue of land inclosed between the two. The older portion has narrow and dirty streets, and an atmosphere of fog and smoke hangs over the city, as in the English manufacturing towns, or as in Pittsburgh and Cincinnati; while the newer portion has wide streets, parks, trees, and blocks of stately buildings.

The next morning after arrival, we set forth to explore the city, refusing all offers of a *commiſsionaire*, having previously thoroughly studied the map and description of it. After visiting the cathedral, we threaded narrow streets, and climbed steep hills, winding between walls of which the form and hight recalled the feudal age, when they were built; paſsed the Hospital of *Antiquailles*, occupying the site of the Roman palace in which Claudius and Caligula were born—which has given way now, by a sort of poetical justice, to an *Hôpital des Incurables*—until we came to the *Chapelle de Fourvieres*, surmounting a high hill which overlooks the town and surrounding country, and even affords, on a clear day, it is said, a view of *Mont Blanc;* but the day was cloudy and the air filled

Chapter I.—Lyons. 5

with smoke and fog, so that we could but dimly discern the city at our feet. The tower of the Chapel is surmounted by a statue of the Virgin, who is said to have stayed the spread of the cholera in Lyons many years ago, while the inner walls, from ceiling to floor, are literally covered with pictures of all sorts and sizes, hung there as votive offerings, in gratitude for special favors granted by the Blefsed Virgin to suffering mortals. Among them are several small copies of the Immaculate Conception, by Murillo, that hangs in the Gallery of the Louvre. There are also a large number of small waxen models of legs and arms, saved to their owners by the Virgin, in answer to their prayers.

After a long walk through other narrow streets, and down steep declivities and long flights of stone steps, we were again on the banks of the Saône, which rushes swiftly through the town, as if impatient to join her stately lord, the Rhone, who waits below; and crofsing the bridge *Fourveueille*, stopped for a moment to look at the women who lined the sides of boats moored along the banks, busily employed in washing clothes. We soon attracted their attention, and, like all French people, desisting from their labors, they indulged in a good, long, full stare at us. I lifted my hat in acknowledgement of their kind attention, and we proceeded on our way, and soon, crossing the *Place des Terreaux*, soaked in the days of the Revolution by the blood of the victims of the guillotine, we entered the Museum. Here are many relics of the Roman age of Lyons; among others, the bronze tables, containing the speech made by Claudius, when Censor, in the Roman Senate, A. D. 48, on the motion that the communities of Gallia Comata should be admitted to the privileges of Roman citizens. The letters are beautifully and clearly cut, and as sharp and legible as if Time had not been pounding at them for eighteen centuries. There are also two or three rooms filled with paintings and drawings of French artists, among which we especially admired some crayon sketches by Menissier, of Metz, exceedingly well done; an *Interior Rustique*, by Bail; *Henri de Guise*, (Balafré) sworn by his mother to revenge his father's death, by Pierre Chas. Comte; *Far Niente*, a picture of an Italian peasant girl, dreamily leaning against a wall in the sunlight; and two small pictures by M'lle Felicié Megret—the one of Galileo in his study—the other of the house of a peasant. There was also a bas-relief worth mentioning, by the Marquis de Parcieu, "*Mignon aspirant au ciel*," after the painting of Ary Scheffer.

In the public square, fronting the Museum, as well as in the Place Imperial and Place de Bellecour, is a beautiful fountain, always playing. The contrast between the old buildings, walls, and streets, on the west of the Saône, and the wide avenues, spacious quays, and lofty, elegant buildings, on such streets as the *Rue Imperiale*, and the quays, is that between old France—venerable with age and laden with the wealth of History accumulated in the progrefs of centuries—and modern France, with the newnefs and lavish elegance that has followed after the

Revolution. The many tints that the hand of History had laid, age by age, upon the canvas of France, were, for the most part, obliterated in the latter part of the seventeenth century, by the brush of the Revolution, soaked in blood, and in Lyons, as in Paris, the marks of antiquity appear more remarkable than those of the present century.

Arising one morning, and looking out the window, we saw one of those sights which a foreign and Catholic country alone affords. Along the quays of the Saône, and the bridge of Tilsit acrofs it, were lines of men, boys, and women, all with wooden shoes, and the women with white caps, anxiously awaiting something that they stretched their necks to see, down the street. The bells of the churches were slowly tolling, and soon appeared a long line of Sisters of Charity, clad in their simple black gowns and white hoods, marching in single file on each side the street. Following these was a great number of priests, bareheaded, bearing lighted candles, the choir in their midst chanting slow, solemn music, with deep bafs voices, accompanied by a brafs instrument, as in the church of St. Roch, in Paris. Next came a coffin, covered with black cloth, fringed with white, borne by men drefsed in black, who were flanked by others, answering to our pall-bearers, all carrying lighted candles. The remainder of the procefsion, which was very long, consisted of citizens, also on foot, but marching close together in pairs, not separated on each side of the street, like the sisters and priests. It was doubtlefs the funeral of some eminent religious person, and was certainly a very strange and picturesque sight for American eyes.

On another day, sitting by our parlor window, looking out upon the quay and the bridge, we saw just below us a vegetable market—an open space where a number of peasant women were selling their cabbages, onions, and similar vegetables. The buyers flock around, and in an hour or two all the articles are sold, and men and women disappear. Picturesque they are—with short dreſses of some dark stuff which knows not crinoline, a huge pair of *sabots* below, and above a sack, or a handkerchief of gay colors, brought round the neck, over the breast, and fastened at the girdle. Some have the white caps worn by a majority of the French women of the lower claſs, and others wear wide flats of straw, with ribbons or without, while here and there appears a head-dreſs of strange form—a flat, round sort of plate, quite large, fastened in some mysterious manner on the top of the head, with a round tower of about two inches in diameter, and three in height, in the center, all covered with a sort of coarse black lace, of which also square flaps, six or eight inches in length, hang at the back of the head.

Men and women walk briskly along, with well filled baskets poised on the tops of their heads. Here goes a man supporting a couple of parallel sticks, one on each side of him, on the ends of which are built up small mountains of boxes; there goes another, in a blue smock frock, pushing before him a large tray, on two wheels, filled with apples

Chapter I.—Lyons.

and oranges for sale; and through the crowd come a couple of priests, with long black gowns, white neckcloths, and wide, black felt hats, turned up at the sides, like the cocked hat of olden times, closely followed, perhaps, by a Zouave, with his dashing little cap, red trowsers and white gaiters. Now, croſsing the bridge, appear the market women on their homeward way, in little two-wheeled carts, drawn by little donkeys; and at the end of the train walks another on foot, leading her little donkey, laden with a couple of large panniers.

Such were some of the sights our windows afforded, while over the river rose the heights of *Fourvières*, where, crowning the highest steeple, stands the gilded statue of the Virgin, stretching out her protecting hand, as if in benison upon the city at her feet.

One morning we engaged a carriage for half a day and drove about the town. After a call upon our banker,—a very courteous old gentleman, head of one of the principal silk-houses,—who received me very politely, and related with great satisfaction that ex-President Van Buren had once sat upon the same sofa that I occupied,—we drove through the park, a tastefully laid out space, adorned with trees and a small lake, on which some swans were swimming; visited the *Jardin des Plantes*, traversed the principal streets, and saw the several squares, with fountains playing in the centres, and finally came home to dine at five o'clock. After dinner we decided to visit the *Grand Théatre*, to see the Barber of Seville, and as it was raining, ordered a carriage. When we descended, our grand carriage, covered now, and the liveried driver, were waiting. It was nearly midnight when we came out from the play, and the rain having ceased, and the stars shining brightly, we decided to walk home, as we had not ordered our carriage to wait. Hardly had we gone two squares, however, when it drove up, and our driver jumped from his box to open the door for us. So we learned that half a day in Lyons lasts from twelve at noon until twelve at night, and that he who pays fifteen francs for a carriage gets the worth of his money.

Early the next morning, before the daylight had appeared, but not before the market women had afsembled and were arranging their vendibles, we rose, and having breakfasted, started for Avignon. A ride of five and a-half hours in the cars, along the right bank of the Rhone, took us thither. By the road runs the rapid river, through a valley cultivated to its utmost extent and capacity, beyond which stand the sentinel mountains, dotted here and there with villages that shine white in the sunlight, and crowned at intervals with castles and chateaux, many of which have long since crumbled into ruins.

Chapter II.—*Avignon*.

ARRIVED at Avignon, we entered an omnibus and drove to the *Hotel de l'Europe*, where we found very comfortable, large rooms, a capital table, attendance and bed. The bread and coffee were excellent, the butter delicious, and the lamb chops fairly melted in the mouth.

Avignon was the ancient city of the Popes, having been conveyed to them by Joanna of Naples, in 1348, although occupied by them, by the invitation of Philip the Fair, from 1305, during the term of their exile from Rome in the fourteenth century, and afterwards by the schismatic Popes for about forty years more. It is still surrounded by lofty walls flanked with watch-towers, and surmounted with battlements, except on the side of the river, where the abrupt cliffs render defense unnecefsary. The streets are paved with small boulders,—(petrified kidneys as some one called them)—on which one must needs do penance in walking, for there are no side-walks—and are lined with low, heavy, whitewashed houses.

The chief attractions are the Palace of the Popes, and the Cathedral adjoining. The former is now used as soldiers' barracks, but the larger portion has been presented by the Emperor to the Archbishop of that diocese, to be delivered as soon as new barracks, now in procefs of erection, shall be completed. "It partakes of the mixed character of a feudal castle and a convent. Its walls are one hundred feet high, and some of its towers one hundred and fifty feet, with a proportionate thicknefs of masonry. It is an edifice rich in afsociations. It was founded by Clement V, in 1309, and during the greater part of the fourteenth century it was the seat of the Papal Court. In those halls, now echoing to the blasphemous oaths of prisoners, or subdivided and filled with soldiers' cribs and accoutrements, the conclave of cardinals sate, by whom the Pope was elected. Here Petrarch was a guest, Giotto and his scholars adorned its walls, and in its dungeon Rienzi was a prisoner."

Here, too, was the chamber of torture for the victims of the Inquisition, and later, in the short life of the French Revolution, deeds of blood were done, from the perusal of which we turn away in horror.

In the Cathedral we saw a chapel of the time of Charlemagne, a tomb of Pope John XXII, whereof the statue, as well as the bones of the Pope, was broken and scattered by the fierce revolutionists, and a statue of the Virgin, by Pradier, very graceful and beautiful. Here also, as in several other churches that we visited, is a representation in figures of the birth of Christ. The infant lies in the cradle, with Joseph and Mary on either side, while at its head stand an ox and an afs, gravely looking down; two or three other figures are added, gener-

Chapter II.—Avignon.

ally of the kings of the east bringing presents, among whom is always a negro, with robe and turban surmounted by a feather.

From the Cathedral, which forms the easternmost portion of the palace, a walk leads into gardens, from which a magnificent view of the fortrefs of Villeneuve, opposite, and of the surrounding country may be obtained. At your feet runs the swift river; beyond it are the villages and the fortres, and still beyond rise the mountains—one covered with perpetual snow—which commence the chain of the Pyrenées. On the other side are Avignon and the plains beyond, dotted with white stone and mortar houses, and strange looking tiled roofs, surrounded by gardens and shaded by trees.

Dismifsing our old *commifsionaire*, we wandered through the narrow, crooked streets. On the hills were olive trees, and in the town were wine shops, with a bush hanging over the door, reminding us of Shakspeare's " Good wine needs no bush." Where white wine is sold, white paper or rags are tied to the bush.

The *mistral*, a strong wind which blows at intervals during the whole year, was prevailing while we were there, but whereas, in summer it is pregnant with discomfort and disease, it was then merely cold, while the sky was without a cloud.

Near the Cathedral is an open square unenclosed, and smoothly graveled, where, at times, the military band plays, and the people gather for promenade and chat. On one side are cafes and shops, and on the other a theatre, with two fine statues flanking its entrance,—one of Moliere and the other of Corneille,—a music hall, formerly the mint of the popes, and between the two the *Hotel de Ville*, a large building surmounted by a clock-tower, in which stand life-size figures of a man and woman, with hammers in their hands, with which they strike the hours.

The Museum contains many relics of the Roman period, and the tomb of Petrarch's Laura,—a crofs, upon which hangs a wreath of flowers, standing on a globe. In the building is a gallery of modern paintings,

Chapter II.—Avignon.

chiefly by artists born at Avignon, but by no means confined to that city. There are three portraits by Grimou, in style resembling the beautiful paintings of Greuze, which no frequenter of the galleries of the Louvre can forget; an exquisite moonlight scene by Vander Neer; Mazeppa pursued by wolves, by Horace Vernet—a most remarkable picture; also paintings by Claude Joseph and Charles Vernet, some of which are very spirited. Best of all, however, are two by French artists, little known in our country,—Évariste Bernardi de Valernes, and Eugéne le Poittevin. By the former there is a Sister of Charity in her conventional drefs, in the face of whom are reflected all the virtues that the poor and needy, and the sick and suffering soldiers of our civil war have learned to asfociate with any member of that order. The latter has Cinderella, sitting in the chimney corner gazing into the fire, seeing in the coals and flames shifting pictures of the bright and beautiful world that young girls all long to enter, but saddened with the thought that she never could realize her dreams. There is a mezzotint of this at Goupil's, in New York, which, though a beautiful picture, conveys but a faint idea of the exquisite original.

Chapter III.—*Nismes—Pont du Gard.*

TWO hours in the cars bring us to Nismes, a beautiful city with wide streets, shady boulevards, superb Roman remains, comfortable looking houses, and last, though not least in the estimation of a traveler, an excellent hotel.

The first visit, of course, was to the *Amphithéatre*—built, as were the other Roman remains, in the days when the town was called *Nemausus*, and was an unimportant city of Gaul. It is of stone, 437 feet long, 332 feet wide at the centre, being oval in form, and 70 feet high—of two stories. There were thirty-two rows of seats, which would accommodate about 20,000 people. Back of the seats are corridors, surrounding the whole building, roofed with huge stones; while the facilities for ingreſs and egreſs would be well worth the study of architects of our easily burned opera houses. It is more perfect, outwardly, than that of Verona, and altogether more so than the Colisseum; and workmen are busily engaged in restoring the portions that have been destroyed.

It was a beautiful morning in February, and the sun was warm enough to tempt us to sit for an hour on the seats, and conjure up the past, when the Roman citizens sat there, patrician and plebian, feasting their eyes upon the deadly struggle of the gladiators, applauding the victor when the cry of "*habet*" rang in the air.

Not far from the Amphithéatre is the *Maison Carrée*, a most perfect and beautiful Corinthian building, which, originally a Roman temple, has paſsed through varied changes—as a Christian church, a city-hall, a stable, a burial house for a convent,—and has finally become a museum. In it are various antiquities; a horrible picture by Sigalon, but one of great power, representing Nero experimenting upon a slave with the poison destined for his brother Britannicus; and a celebrated and much more interesting painting, by Paul Delaroche, of Cromwell holding open the coffin-lid of Charles I, and gazing on the features of the dead king. By Guido, is a Judith, at the moment when, attired in her richest robes, she is told that it is time to go to Holofernes. Her face is very beautiful, and her dreamy eyes and smooth brow would seem to show that she was thinking more of the coming conquest of her beauty, and of the consequent triumph among her people, than of the dreadful deed she was on the eve of undertaking.

The other most noticeable thing in the Museum is a statue of The Dancing Girl, by Pradier. In one hand she holds a harp; the other is raised; her head, and the upper portion of her body are thrown back, the mouth half open, as if singing; one foot slightly advanced; the other leg and foot covered with the mantle which has just fallen from her shoulders, leaving the form nude. Her figure is lithe, beautifully rounded, perfectly formed and in graceful pose, making altogether one of the most exquisite statues I saw in Europe.

In the public square, close by, is another work of Pradier—a marble fountain; on each of the four sides of which is a figure, representing four rivers, presiding over the four streams of crystal water that issue from the marble. This is surmounted by a lofty and commanding female statue wearing a crown, representing on one side the *Maison Carrée*, and on the other the *Amphithéatre*. It is a striking work, and especially effective by moonlight.

Back of the town rises a hill of considerable height, on which stands a hollow, conical shaped structure, much battered by time, called *La Tour Magne*, supposed to have been a Roman tomb. We climbed the circular staircase, in its interior, to the summit, and were rewarded with a magnificent and extended prospect, including the Pyrenées, the fertile valley, the city, with its ancient buildings prominent, and its gardens and long rows of trees; while afar to the left the white, dim, cloudy looking shapes above the horizon are, the old guide says, the snow-clad Alps, and the glimmering light on the southern horizon is that of the sea. When we had descended, and bought of the old grey-moustached keeper a few photographs, raising his hat most courteously, he offered my wife her choice of card-photographs as a present "*si votre mari permittra.*" She chose one of the tower, and we parted in high good humor.

At the foot of the hill a copious fountain bursts from its side, which flows into a large reservoir of cut stone, with a fountain in the centre. These are supposed to have been used by the Romans as baths for women. By the side of the baths is a ruined temple of Diana, and beyond stretch gardens which are the pride of this most interesting city.

On the hill-side we saw a soldier and a peasant girl enjoying a lunch, with the inevitable bottle of red wine, and wondered if "the old, old story was told again" there, as it has been at so many other times and places since Adam and Eve talked in the garden.

In the entrance to the gardens was a bridal party of young peasants, the bride all in white, with veil and orange blofsom wreath, and the bridegroom in traditional black suit and white cravat. It is sometimes comforting to think that Adam, with all his troubles, was saved the necefsity of black drefs and white cravat when he was married. Further on was a procefsion of young priests, still in the shell, but with big hats, long gowns, white cravats and low shoes, as if they were already full fledged; and still further down the street were Punch and Judy, scolding and cracking crowns, and amusing the crowd with English vigor and French vivacity. We sat down for half an hour, on a bench under the trees, to watch the crowd, ostensibly, but I fear that Mr. Punch came in for half the watching.

It rained heavily when we arose one

Chapter III.—Nismes, Pont du Gard.

morning in Nismes, insomuch that we decided to forego the pleasure of a visit to the *Pont du Gard*, a remnant of an ancient Roman aqueduct, about fifteen miles distant; but after breakfast the clouds broke away, the sun came forth warm as in April, so the trunks were unstrapped again and a carriage ordered.

So in an open carriage, through fields of olive trees covered with their rich green leaves, past almond trees clothed in white robes of blofsom, past old-looking tile-roofed houses, against the walls of which were trained rose-bushes, already heavy with flowers, past stone crofses and ruined chateaux, with a good road beneath, and a sky as blue as ever summer showed above, with horses which trotted fast under the combined incentives of jingling bells, and the incefsant cracking of the driver's whip, now and then rolling through a sleepy old village, furnishing thereby much excitement to the inhabitants, who all came out to stare at us, we drove to the promised ruins. And well were we repaid. A tier of six mafsive arches, spanning a deep ravine, at the bottom of which runs a shallow stream, and supporting a wide bridge and a second tier of eleven arches, smaller than the first, but still grand in size; which in turn supports a third tier of thirty-five still smaller arches; which last are surmounted by the aqueduct—so wide that two people can easily walk abreast in it, and nearly five feet in depth! Imagine all this—built of mafsive stone, of plain and severe architecture, in a wild, though beautiful country, with scarcely a human habitation in sight— 180 feet high and 870 in length, built 1600 years ago; a portion of an aqueduct which brought water twenty-five miles to Nismes, —and you may have some idea of its grandeur, and of the magnificence of the people for whom it was built.

The day was one of uninterrupted pleasure—the ride, the sight, the lunch at the way-side inn, of bread and cheese and sparkling sour wine—and as we were approaching the city on our return, the setting sun touched the clouds with his masterhand, and gave us a glorious picture.

Chapter IV.

Toulouse—Bordeaux—Pau—Bayonne.

FROM Nismes by rail to Toulouse, is not a long ride; and as we hurried along, our thoughts fled away into the past, and we mingled with the gay crowd and listened to the song of the troubadour. But the glory that gilded the city in those days has become rusty and dim; and a city not handsome or attractive in itself, with a hotel about every nook and cranny of which hung an odor which was neither of sanctity nor roses, soon drove fair ladies, and gallant knights, and troubadours, and all, from our minds, which were straightway filled with plans for getting away, that were soon formed and put into operation.

As we entered the car, *en route* for Bordeaux, there were four gentlemen, evidently of one party, who sat each at a window, leaving the four seats in the middle of the compartment vacant. After a few minutes one of the gentlemen rose and offered my wife his place. She declined taking it. Another rose and begged her to take his, and then the third and fourth followed. Finally one of them changed his seat and would not be satisfied until she took the place he had left. This last was a very intelligent and pleasant gentleman, and we kept up a long conversation. By the way, nothing strikes an American traveler more than the custom in France, and particularly in Spain, of each man, on entering or leaving a car, raising his hat and bowing politely to his fellow travelers, and immediately offering to converse with his neighbor.

We went through the valley of the Garonne, one of the most beautiful in France, fully one half of which, however, was under water, caused by rains, said to have been

Chapter IV.—Toulouse to Bayonne.

heavier than at any time for one hundred years.

It is remarkably fertile, and, as is common in France, the land is nearly all owned by peasants, who buy strips of ten to fifty feet in width, and from one to three hundred feet in depth. As soon as a peasant collects a few hundred francs he buys a little strip of ground with it, and raises a few vegetables and vines, some owning but a single furrow.

Bordeaux is a truly lordly city, with its broad stone quays,—said to be the finest in the world—beautiful gardens, lofty buildings, and its Cathedral, through the exquisitely painted windows of which streams the varied colored light.

The gardens are large and tastefully laid out, with a stream running through them almost literally filled with gold fish, and adorned with numerous fountains, groves of various trees, and parterres of brilliant flowers ; and on Sunday afternoon one may see hundreds of people walking about the avenues, listening to the music of the band, watching the swans or the gold fish, or the large number of children who in a broad open graveled space are busy with their games.

There is an Art Museum, but its treasures are few,—a couple of Grimoux, a beautiful Achenbach, a Claude, and a remarkable painting, by Cogniet, of Tintoret painting the portrait of his dead daughter, comprise the best of the collection. There are many others, which they told us were Titian's, Rubens', Rembrandt's, Van Dyke's, and the like, but we took the liberty of disbelieving what they told us, out of respect to those great names.

We had a capital hotel near the quay,— the *Hotel de Nantes*—about which will ever linger for me the delicious perfume of La Tour Blanche and Château Margaux.

I was struck with the difference between the hours of businefs here and those prevalent in England and our own country. Calling on my banker, who had one of the largest houses in the city, about one in the afternoon, I was told no one was in, but I could call at three and find the partners.

Chapter IV.—Toulouse to Bayonne.

Subsequently I inquired their office hours, "From nine to twelve" was the reply, and "from half-past past two till six." "But why this closing for two hours in the middle of the day?" "Ah, monsieur, we go to take our breakfast!"

Leaving Bordeaux, we proceeded southward to Bayonne, stopping *en route* at Pau, for two or three days, to see some friends from home. Hitherto we had been presided over by a special genius of the weather, for we took clear skies with us wherever we went, and were becoming something of fatalists in our belief in our good luck, but at Pau the presiding genius of the place triumphed over ours, and the rain was almost incefsant during our stay. In spite of that, however, we drove along the banks of the beautiful *Gave*, and among the hills, which gave promise of great beauty when the leaves should clothe the trees, and the sun should shine again, lamenting only those lines of stunted and deformed trees of which the beauty and grace had fallen victims to the necefsity for faggots.

It was a pleasure which only those can realize who for several months have not seen one familiar face, to meet and mingle with friends, and discuſs home news and home scenes, but on the third day, having had a glimpse of the fine scenery afforded by a few hours of sunshine, and wandered through the castle of Henry IV, the great hero of those parts, and thought of Bernadotte, who went from thence a drummer-boy and died King of Sweden, we proceeded to Bayonne, a lively town, but of little interest to us, save for its fortifications, a curious old cathedral, and an exquisite church of modern architecture, which at the time of our visit was all dreſsed with flowers for some festival.

Here we found a courier named Mariano, a Spanish merchant formerly, and well to do, but now poor, and making his bread and butter by acting sometimes as courier, and at others as an *employé* of the British Consul at Bayonne. Honest and truthful as a gentleman, economical to a fault, and simple as a child, poſseſsed of the French,

Chapter IV.—Toulouse to Bayonne.

Spanish and English languages, attentive and active, he was a gem—nay, a very *Koh-i-noor* of a courier. But the poor fellow had once had a sun-stroke, which affected his brain in some degree, and at Madrid the rarity of the air and the excitement of the city affected him so that I was compelled, though reluctantly, to send him back to Bayonne. I afterwards engaged Manuel Bazan, who is recommended by Fetridge, in Harper's Handbook of Travel, in whose recommendation, after two months' trial, I most heartily concur.

The road from Bordeaux to Bayonne runs nearly the whole distance through a flat, sandy pine barren, called *Les Grandes Landes*. Scarcely any houses are to be seen, excepting in the few villages on the route, but everywhere the pine and fir trees, with patches of grafs here and there, which serve as sheep pastures. The shepherds of this region, instead of the traditional pipe and crook, have a pair of lofty stilts, and a long staff with a piece nailed across the top. These stilts answer the double purpose of keeping them out of the sand, and as posts of observation, while the staff is for sitting on without dismounting. The traveler, as he speeds along, will generally see two or three of these strange looking tripods together, conversing and knitting.

The region is said to have been comparatively bare at a former period, but proving an excellent place for the cultivation of evergreens, they have been planted in great numbers. It is also said that the Emperor is largely interested in this section, and when North Carolina seceded and the products of her pine forests rose so rapidly in value, the Imperial speculator realized a handsome profit from his venture.

Chapter V.—*Irun—Burgos.*

AT noon we left Bayonne, by rail, for Burgos, expecting to reach that place at midnight. But human plans "gang aft aglee." And so did ours on this occasion, Bradshaw to the contrary notwithstanding.

At Irun, the first Spanish station, we changed cars, and sat patiently for an hour, waiting until the gentry in blue and red uniforms, and light straw-colored caps, black moustaches, cigarettes, and dirty fingers, had finished searching our baggage. The trunks were very small, and perhaps therefore the more suspicious, or perhaps the hour before the train would leave was to be filled up some how or other, and this presented a tempting method of so doing; but whatever the reason, most certain it is that our trunks were most thoroughly searched that day.

Clothes were carefully shaken, parcels of gloves unwrapped, brushes examined, and nothing contraband discovered, until a box was found which seemingly presented no means of opening it. The officer turned it about and around, looked at its top and bottom, shook it, and at last unable to comprehend the secret, handed it to our courier and asked what it was. He did not know, and asked us. I would not tell. How to get it open, and its contents, the officer must discover for himself. His temper did not seem to be improved by this, but he was amusing us, and I had no idea of losing the amusement. So he pulled, and worked, and shook, and at last seized with a brilliant idea unscrewed the top, and found inside a bottle. He opened the bottle and smelt of its contents, but did not recognise the perfume. He asked Mariano what it was. Mariano did not know, and I refused to tell. Up went the bottle to his nose again, but gaining no information by that means, he tasted it. Having done so he spat on the ground with disgust, and looking very savagely at us, who were much amused, put in the stopper, screwed up the cover, and put it back. The bottle contained *hair wash!*

Soon after he brought forth a small long newspaper parcel, containing two round barrels. Here was something wrong. Now he could bring *los Americanos* to grief, and eagerly untwisted the ends of the paper, unrolled it and discovered—two candles, which, in a fit of disgust at the Toulouse hotel bill, we had carried off and forgotten all about.

His official sternnefs melted into surprise, and as his eyebrows rose, Mariano's mouth expanded, and we burst into a hearty laugh.

At last we were off again, but in the afternoon were detained a couple of hours at a way-station, waiting for a train, and finally about one in the morning, we were aroused from sleep by cries and the glare of torches. Whether the cars were on fire or robbers had attacked the train, or Burgos was reached, we could not tell, but in a moment came the pleasing intelligence that a tunnel had fallen in and we must walk over the mountain.

There was no help for it! so we set forth. Up, up, up we went, until the climbing had nearly taken away our breath, while still above us, and far below, flared the great torches and sounded the cries of the Spanish guides who lighted our path and carried the baggage on their shoulders.

Up still until we reached the summit, where the cold wintry wind blew strongly and bit shrewdly. Far down below lay the train we had left; all up the side of the mountain the torches flared in the wind; by our side stood a guide, with ragged brown pantaloons, leather leggins, slouched hat, and a cloak like unto Joseph's, for variety of color, and to the famous boots of Peter the Great for composition, while away down in the valley below shone the lamp of the engine of the train that was to carry us on.

Not a shrub, nor a tree, was to be seen as far as the moonlight allowed the eye to reach ; and as the torches lit up the motley line of travelers, and guides, and porters, and glistened on the arms of the guards who walked at the side of the procefsion, muffled in their cloaks, with their black eyes peering from under their cocked hats, I thought I had never beheld a scene so wild and picturesque.

But it was too cold to stand there long, and therefore down the other side of the mountain, by a zig-zag path so steep that for half the distance we descended by steps cut in the earth, to the new train, which in an hour more took us to Burgos.

This ancient city, once the proud capital of proud Castile, renowned by the deeds of the Count Fernan Gonzales, and the Cid so famed in story and in song, losing somewhat of its greatnefs by the removal of the Court to Toledo, in the eleventh century, is now a dull, quiet, sleepy town, with narrow crooked streets, containing about 25,000 inhabitants, and is interesting to the traveler chiefly on account of its Cathedral.

This Gothic structure, about three hundred feet in length, by an average breadth of ninety-three feet, rich in carving and ornament, is unfortunately situated on uneven ground, and much obscured by surrounding buildings. In the interior it is divided into three naves, separated by rows of pillars. The effect of the length, however, as in all the Spanish Cathedrals, is greatly injured by the situation of the high altar and choir, which are placed in the center of the church, instead of at one end as with us. It is built of very light colored stone and appears within as if it were of comparatively recent erection, although it has been standing about six hundred years. There are neither chairs nor pews in any of the Cathedrals in Spain, but all the worshippers kneel on the stone floor, the women generally afsuming a squatting position when not actually engaged in prayer. They are

Chapter V.—Irun—Burgos.

most democratic institutions ; the ragged beggar boy, that Murillo delighted to paint, may be seen kneeling by the side of the lady whose rich black drefs and fine lace mantilla give evidence of pofsefsion of wealth, and the workman and the titled are on an equality there.

When the French blew up the castle in 1813, the Cathedral was not injured, contrary to general expectation, but the beautifully painted glafs windows were all destroyed.

The towers, which are three hundred feet high, are triumphs of art—so light one wonders they are not blown away in that stormy region ; and so open one can see the stars through them at night. Viewed from a distance they are exceedingly beautiful.

There is, of course, much to admire in a building almost encrusted with statues and carving, but one of the most interesting objects is the carved wood forming the seats of the choir. This is wrought into all manner of strange shapes, while there are two tiers of bas-reliefs, representing scenes from the Old and New Testament, all exquisitely finished, while in the centre is an inlaid seat, representing, strangely enough, the rape of Europa!

The chest of the Cid is shown by the sacristan,—an old wooden iron-bound box, in which the brave Rodrigo kept his treasures. But once when he was going on an expedition, his exchequer was very low, so he sent for two wealthy Jews to dine with him, and warming them with wine, proposed to borrow of them the sum required, depositing in their keeping his chest, which he afsured them was filled with plate, and gold, and jewels. The box was very heavy, and the Cid's word was supposed to be very good, so the Jews lent him the money, without opening the box. Afterward, the Cid being succefsful in his expedition and acquiring much spoil, returned this money, and apologized for the fact that the box contained only sand.

For this he is lauded by the Spanish chroniclers; for the reason I suppose that he was honest enough to pay what he had dishonestly borrowed, a thing perhaps of infrequent occurrence in Spain.

Around a clock in the corner may generally be found a small collection of people, waiting for the striking of the hour, when an Apostle steps forth, and after striking the four quarters on a little bell, retires, closing the doors after him, upon which a grotesque figure strikes the hour on a large bell, opening his mouth from ear to ear at each stroke.

In one of the chapels we saw the Christ of Burgos,—a most admirable work of art, —carved, as the legend runs, by Nicodemus, out of supernatural wood, so that none can say what it is, and found by a merchant of Burgos in the Bay of Biscay, whither it had come of its own accord from the East; and pofsefsed of the power of working miracles. The effect, however, is much injured by one of the stiff silk petticoats, embroidered with gold, with which the Spaniards generally drape the figure.

Not far from the city is a hill, on the

brow of which stands the citadel. We climbed up to it in the morning, and finding no officer of whom to ask leave, walked in, and acrofs to the ramparts, whence we had a fine view of the surrounding country and the city at our feet, with the lofty towers of the Cathedral overtopping all. After we had been there about half an hour, the commandant sent word that as we had entered without asking permifsion, we must retire immediately, and as we had seen all we cared to, we cheerfully obeyed; and taking a carriage drove to the convent *La Cartuja*, about three miles from the city, to see the tombs of Juan II, and Isabella of Portugal.

These wonderful mausoleums are octagonal in shape, guarded at each corner by two lions, that support escutcheons on which are carved the royal arms. All the sides are covered with delicate carvings of figures under filagree canopies, fruit, openworked leaves, birds, animals, and other objects, of perfect form and harmony. On the tops lie the full length figures of the king and queen, with life-like features and most wonderfully worked robes and laces. At the feet of the queen a lion, child, and dog are lying. All these are carved in alabaster, and defy description.

Near by, in a recefs in the wall, is the statue of Don Alonso, their son, (also of life size,) who is represented kneeling on a cushion. Over him is a Gothic arch, festooned with a grape vine, the whole, like the others, presenting numberlefs leaves, flowers, and figures of exquisite workmanship. This, also, is all of alabaster. They were placed there towards the close of the fifteenth century, by Queen Isabella, the sister of the Infanta.

The sights I have mentioned comprise the chief attractions of Burgos; and our hotel, dirty and uncomfortable, the weather very cold, with only a brazier of charcoal and ashes to warm ourselves with, (for there are no fire-places in Spain, except in a few new hotels,) induced us to linger no longer, but push on to Valladolid, where the chances for comfortable housing might be better. We did so, but after a sleep and a breakfast we decided not to spend another night there, for we had come from the frying-pan to the fire.

Chapter VI.—*Valladolid—Escorial.*

AND indeed, one day is sufficient to see all that Valladolid offers. Situated on a wide plain, the cold winds have free course in winter, and the Spaniards who were walking on the Prado when we went to see it, must have been taking a serious constitutional.

Philip II, who was born here, did much to embellish and adorn it while it still remained the Capital of Spain, and it was a large and flourishing city. After he removed his Court to Madrid, however, the population diminished, and the city has now 43,000 inhabitants.

We rambled about the dead old town, with its crooked streets and white buildings, old churches, and dirty beggars, crouched in the corners where the sun had most power, until we came to the Museum, which, among many pictures, statues, and other objects, contains few worthy of notice, and fewer still to be recollected. The most curious of all was a considerable series of pictures, representing various scenes in the life of Christ, in which all the prominent figures are made of mother-of-pearl. The authorship is unknown, but they are said to be of great antiquity.

While walking on the Prado I gave a beggar a copper. "Don't, for God's sake, Mr. M.," said our old guide. "If you give to one, they will smell you a mile." And in truth, they were plentiful enough. One ludicrous instance occurred. Two blind men sat on one side of the street. On our approach a little girl was sent acrofs to beg. She, mistaking her instructions, accosted two Spaniards in front of us, which the blind men *seeing*, called out to her to cease and turn to us, which she did, with the usual "*por amor Dios, Señor*," but which only

Chapter VI.—Valladolid—Escorial.

provoked laughter on this occasion, and the reply, "*Vaya con Dios,*" which turns away a Spanish beggar about as surely as a soft answer turneth away wrath.

From Valladolid we went by rail to the village of Escorial, about twenty miles from Madrid, arriving about five o'clock in the morning, and were glad to find a comfortable bed, and a good breakfast afterwards.

At a short distance is the famous palace of the Escorial, the reflex, in stone, of the character of its half-monk, half-king, builder, Philip II. Built of granite, with long corridors of low, flattened arches, of immense size, in a rocky, desolate region, it is as gloomy an abode as even its royal owner could desire.

Pafsing through the principal entrance, over which are placed colofsal figures of the six kings of Judea who are said to have afsisted in the building of Solomon's Temple—all of granite, with heads and hands of white marble—we proceeded directly to the Church. This is also granite, of the Doric style, and the greatest simplicity, but of in-

exprefsible grandeur. It is of large size—
320 feet long, 230 feet broad, and 320 feet
to the top of the cupola; but the secret of
its grandeur is in its perfect proportion and
severe simplicity. The Cathedrals of Burgos and Toledo are more rich in carvings
and more gorgeous in appearance; that of
Seville is greater in size and adorned with
world-famous paintings; those of Cologne
and Milan more beautiful, and St. Peter's
more vast and better suited for the capital
where the head of the church may lead in
worship, and all the gorgeous ceremonies
of the Catholic Church be performed;
but more in this than in any other did
I feel that sense of awe which he felt of
old who knelt in the very Holy of
Holies. If ever there was a temple
where one must hold his breath and feel
that "God alone is great," it surely is
this.

Immediately under the altar, which is
composed of the variously colored marbles,
is the dome of the tomb, curiously named
the Pantheon, an octagonal chamber, of

highly polished marble, on shelves about the sides of which are metallic coffins, inclosed in porphyry urns, in which rest the bodies of the kings and queens of Spain, placed there in fulfillment of the vow of Philip II, to have high mafs said for their souls, over their bodies, every day.

The palace is exquisitely fitted up with inlaid woods, gilding and tapestry, and was formerly the repository of many fine paintings, of which, however, but few are now left, the remainder having been transferred to the Museum at Madrid. At last, after inspecting the Convent, we visited the rooms of the king who built all this. A small antechamber, or salon, where he received his ambafsadors, a narrow, dark, unventilated bed-room, and a small study, where are his chair, the support for his gouty foot, and his writing materials, all of the plainest sort,—all the rooms having earthenware floors and walls of blue Dutch tiles,—form the apartments he delighted to occupy. Close beside them is a narrow recefs, from which a small door opens into the church, where died this singular compound of pride and self-abasement, cool ferocity and superstitious piety—who deceived his friends and confeſsed his sins daily, and deluged the land in blood for the glory of God and the honor of his royal line.

The building was erected both in compliance with the wish of Charles V, and in fulfillment of a vow to St. Laurence, on whose day the victory of St. Quentin was won, and being a rectangular parallelogram, with long corridors and a tower at each corner, is thought to have been purposely constructed in the form of a reversed gridiron, in honor of the method of martyrdom of that saint.

After spending the whole day in this wonderful pile, we returned to the hotel, and after dining, again took the cars, arriving at Madrid about nine o'clock, when we drove to the *Grand Hotel de Paris*, the largest and best hotel in the city, situated on the *Puerta del Sol*.

Chapter VII.—*Madrid.*

ON inquiring for rooms we were shown two on the first floor, (or second story in our understanding,) which seemed very pleasant, but had no fire-place. These were six dollars per day. On the floor above, we found two others with a fire-place, which were *eight* dollars a day; but they were on the shady side of the house, and consequently very cold, and we subsequently changed to two others on the floor below, on the sunny side, for which we paid *ten* dollars per day,—or, as I estimated it, six for the rooms, two for fire-place, and two for sunshine. These prices include dinner, and breakfast of eggs, wine and bread. As an Englishman once said to me, "He who wishes coffee, champagne and such luxuries must expect to pay for them," as well as for fire, lights, service, and other extras.

But it was a very comfortable house, and for the first time since leaving Bayonne we luxuriated in an open fire-place with a blazing fire in it, and soon lost the colds contracted on the way thither.

Every one has read of Madrid,—its *Puerta del Sol*, the lounging place of all claſses of people,—its Prado, lined with trees, with carriage road and broad sidewalks, where, on pleasant afternoons, the Madrilenians may be seen walking or driving; the palace, a vast stone structure of fine architectural effect; its museums and its galleries of paintings; and I shall rather endeavor to give an idea of our life there, and the strange and beautiful sights we saw, than of the appearance of the city itself.

Of course our first walk on the morning after our arrival, (after a visit to my banker's for letters,) was to the Gallery of Paintings, whither we resorted almost daily during our stay, and always with increasing pleasure.

This collection, begun by Charles V and Philip II, the friends and patrons of Rubens, Titian and Velasquez, and afterwards largely increased by Philip IV and Philip V, is one of the most attractive, as it is said to be one of the finest galleries in the world, in which opinion, after seeing those of Rome, Florence and Dresden, I concur. From the Netherlands, from Italy, and from France, they drew their treasures, and when the Commonwealth of England sold the Van Dykes and other gems of the collection of Charles I, Spain was a large purchaser, and in that dry, conservative climate, time deals gently with works of art.

Besides the Raphaels, Rubens, Titians, Tintorettos, Paul Veroneses, Claudes, Van Dykes,—all of whom are represented by some of their best works, and large numbers of Teniers, Wouvermans, Both, and many other well known artists,—is a larger collection of Spanish masters than is to be found in any other place in the world. Zurbaran, Ribera, Valasquez, and Murillo, can be studied to more advantage here than in any other place. Indeed, nearly all of the works of Velasquez are to be found here, and more of Murillo's best than elsewhere, excepting at Seville.

It would need a better art critic than myself, to comment on the riches that cover the walls, so as to describe without wearying the reader. One has literally *embarras de richesse*. But the "Pearl" of Raphael; a "Conception" by Murillo—who, if ever painter drank of the cup of inspiration, had quaffed largely ere he so painted purity and innocence itself, enshrined in beauty—the child Christ giving his playmate, St. John, to drink from a shell, by the side of the stream; the Magdalen, weary with watching, and worn with grief; Rebecca at the well; and others by the same master; Titian's Charles V, on horseback; Valasquez' wonderful portraits of the royal family of Spain; Tintoretto's Shipwreck, from out which looks a woman's face of remarkable beauty; and four exquisite Claudes, would of themselves well repay the lover of art for a journey to Madrid.

We visited, one morning, the Royal Armory, where we saw the armor of Charles V, Philip II, Isabella I,—as well as those of other celebrated characters,—but most interesting of all, to us, that of Cortez and Christopher Columbus, in which we believed firmly, caring naught for historic doubts suggested by sceptical guide-books. Here, also, we saw the swords of Ferdinand and Isabella; of Don John, hero of Lepanto; of Pizarro, conqueror of Peru; of Cortes, and of the unfortunate Boabdil, last Moorish sovereign of Grenada.

The Palace we could not enter, as the royal family were residing there during the period of our stay. We often saw the Queen,—a fat, sensual looking woman, whose appearance by no means contradicts the general report of her character,—in an open carriage, accompanied by the King, her husband, who has rather an intellectual face, and was constantly bowing to those upon the sidewalks, who raised their hats as they pafsed. The carriage was drawn by eight or ten horses, preceded by a company of mounted guards, with brafs helmets and flowing horse-hair plumes, and followed by another carriage containing the children. The young Prince and heir to the throne is a very dark, black eyed, active boy, of intelligent countenance, and seemingly remarkable only on account of his position, and for being the son of such a mother.

The royal stables are large and interesting. Some three hundred horses, including several American brood mares, English, Arabian, and Spanish horses, and about two hundred mules, are kept there, and adjoining is the carriage house, where are the magnificent but heavy, lumbering state coaches.

We frequently visited the theatres, and one evening saw a spectacle called 1864 and 1865. The former, as an old man with long white beard and hair, shows the latter, —a man ludicrously arrayed as a child, who is taken out of a cradle—the various

Chapter VII.—Madrid.

matters and things which it is necefsary for him to encounter during his life. The steam-engine pafses, and the telegraph and the printing prefs, and other motive powers of the world. Then appears a man bearing a banner, half of which is torn off, labeled "Spanish credit." Next is seen the front of the existing Academy of Art,—Murillo and Valasquez pafsing by, suddenly stop, read the sign, raise their hands in horror, and rush from the stage. Various other tableaux succeed, and finally appears a statue of Liberty, draped in mourning. People of different clafses pafs by, when the statue glides away, and in a moment there rushes on the stage a genuine street mob, composed of people from all ranks of life, the gentleman, artisan, and beggar, armed with all manner of weapons, led by a small man in his shirt-sleeves, waving a sword, and all shouting *Libertad, Libertad*, while the orchestra plays the Marseillaise.

The excitement of the audience was intense. Handkerchiefs waved, hats were thrown into the air, *vivas* were shouted.

and three times the scene was repeated with equal enthusiasm.

Upon inquiry why such demonstrations were not stopped by the government, I was informed that at first the government affected to laugh at it, but afterward a number of other theatres took up the play, and the excitement was so general and great that it was feared the threatened revolt would be hastened by endeavor to put down the representations. Great difsatisfaction certainly exists, and it is evident that the time must come when the present government must accept liberal ideas, or be overwhelmed by the march of humanity.

I was amused one day by the title of one of the plays — *Pan y Toros* — "bread and bulls,"—which seem to be the necefsities of Spanish life at present, as were *Panis et Circenses*, — " bread and games" — to the Romans, or "bread and circuses" to young America.

We attended a bull-fight during the Carnival season at Madrid, at which, although it was not a *regular* bull-fight, there were five bulls and seven horses killed, but unfortunately, in the estimation of the Spaniards, no man. It is certainly an exciting scene, but exceedingly barbarous and cruel. One horse, after being gored on each side so that his entrails dragged on the ground, was still ridden around the ring to seek a fresh encounter. This, however, became too much even for the Spaniards, and he was ordered out of the ring by the Alcalde, or governor of the city, who always presides on such occasions. The horses employed are veritable "crow-baits," and so long as they are in the ring your sympathies are all with them; but after they leave they are entirely with the bull, and I could not help agreeing with an English gentleman who accompanied us, who "wished the bull would catch that rascal in yellow."

The bull-fight has been so often described that it would be uselefs for me to attempt it. Some of the feats are full of daring, and exhibit great skill and agility, and are very exciting; but I think it can scarcely be a matter of doubt that such exhibitions must necefsarily exercise a pernicious influence upon the people. All clafses, of both sexes, attend regularly, and therefore all partake of the taint, which among a lazy, ignorant, pleasure-loving and pleasure-seeking people, must be much greater than among a different population.

The ignorance of all clafses in Spain is remarkable. I was asked if America was part of England, by a well-to-do shopkeeper; and I could fill a page with such remarks, by people of the best social position, which were told me while we were in Madrid, by those who had lived there a long time, and the peasants, who bear the reputation of being the most honest clafs, are wonderfully ignorant.

The life of a woman of fashion is divided between eating, drinking, sleeping, driving on the Prado, the theatre, opera and balls. Men who have enough to enable them to live plainly and drefs well, lounge about all day, smoking cigarettes, and haunt the theatres and cafés at night. It is an old maxim that idleneſs is the parent of vice, and the family is consequently very numerous. The clergy, provided with immense revenues, largely choose their profeſsion for the means of livelihood; and while they discharge the duties required by the forms of the church, care nothing for the education of their flocks, as witneſs the statistics —which show that out of a population of about 16,000,000, three-fourths, or 12,000,000, can neither read nor write. With ignorance travel poverty and crime, and Spain—blefsed with fertile soil, fine climate, rich stores of minerals, coals and marbles—groans under the curses of want of intelligence, want of good government, and want of religion. Let the cause of education be really undertaken in earnest, the government liberalized and reformed, and the church purified, and Spain may yet regain her proud position among the Catholic powers of Europe.

We accompanied Mrs. Perry—wife of our Secretary of Legation—one afternoon, to the Hall of the Cortes, (the meaning of which word is *courteous*,) to hear the debates. The general style was most decorous. All the members were well drefsed, and sat with their gloves on—as we would do at a theatre—evidently debating some question concerning which was much excitement; but their conduct of it would be a good model for some of our Southern brethren in Congrefs—even the valiant Roufseau, or his Egyptian opponent, or the poetical Cooper.

The days pafsed rapidly, and when evening came, and dinner was over, there generally gathered in our sitting-room Mr. W., Col. F., and Capt. H.—three English gentlemen—to discufs a cup of real English breakfast tea, which we had taken the precaution to bring a supply of from England. Many were the political discufsions, the anecdotes of people, and manners in Spain, Portugal and Fayal, in which Col. F. had had many adventures; and many were the cigars and cups of tea that vanished in those pleasant evenings. One story of the Colonel's is worth preserving for its singularity:

Chapter VII.—Madrid.

"There grows in Catalonia a weed that will make the fortune of him who shall discover it, for it will eat iron, and cut into the strongest bars in the smallest space of time. Once upon a time, some boys were hunting birds' nests, and they came upon one wherein were some rare and beautiful birds. Afraid to disturb them, one watched while the other went for a cover of iron wire to put over the nest, so as to keep them (the birds) prisoners until a cage could be procured. The cover was brought and put carefully over the nest, and the boys retired in great glee. The next day they returned with a cage, but their cover was gone, and the birds as well. Wonderingly, they searched the ground at the foot of the tree for the cover, but found only some bits of wire. Some weeds were lying about also, and happening to touch the wire with a weed, it straightway fell into two pieces, and the secret was discovered. Other birds, friends of the prisoners, discovering their distrefs, had brought this wonderful weed, and laid it upon the cover, which, falling to pieces, left them free. But where the weed came from no one knows to this day, and the discovery is yet reserved for some fortunate man."

The hours in Madrid are later than in any capital I have seen. Long after midnight the roar of carriages, and the cries of newsboys, peddlers and others, rise from the street, so loud that if one shut his eyes it would be easier to imagine himself in New York, at noon of day, than in a city at noon of night. Business, the hotels, and every body, must conform; and one morning, when about nine o'clock, I rang the bell and inquired what they had for breakfast, the answer was: "They have not come from market yet, sir. I don't know what we *will* have."

On Sunday commenced the Carnival. For two or three days previous had the tomtoms sounded in the streets; but now began the real masquerade. Companies of men, in almost every imaginable variety of costume, paraded the streets; some with brass bands, some with flutes and tambourines, some with bag-pipes, and some with castanets; stopping here and there in the crowded street to dance, while the scouts, with their caps or tambourines, begged from all paſsers; jumping on the steps of carriages, putting their arms around the men and women they met, calling to the spectators who crowded the windows, and carefully collecting any amount of copper coins which were thrown to them. The *Calle Alcalá*, a street leading to the Prado, was thronged with carriages, and the Prado and the principal streets filled with all manner of people, masked or unmasked, on foot, on horseback, or in carriages. It was one constant, universal frolic, and so continued, with masked balls at night, for three days, when the Lenten season commenced.

Chapter VIII.—*Toledo—La Mancha*.

LEAVING Madrid in the afternoon, paſsing through Aranjuez *en route*, we arrived at Toledo at ten P. M., and were conveyed by the one solitary omnibus of the town to our hotel, where we got tolerably comfortable beds and meals, but, for the first time, no butter. One can always find excellent chocolate, bread, salad, and generally a good cutlet or chop, however, wherever he goes.

The sun was very warm the next day, when we set out for the sword manufactory on the plain below the city, about half an hour's walk,—but if we had chosen to ride we could not have done so, for carriages are not to be obtained. We walked, therefore,

Chapter VIII.—Toledo—La Mancha.

and went through the building, seeing the various proceſses of manufacture, and the elastic blades that bend in circles without breaking.

On the way back, we visited the old Roman Amphithéatre, now but a maſs of ruins, croſsed the old Roman bridge, and mounted the hill on which the city stands, preceded by a water-carrier, driving a couple of donkeys loaded with panniers full of jars of water. He sang one of those peculiarly monotonous, plaintive songs to be heard in Spain, and was lazily walking and watching the strangers. Nearly all the music of Spain has a burthen of sorrow, as if the loſs of its former greatneſs had unconsciously saddened its people.

We visited old Moorish houses, with their singular ceilings and tiled walls, and courts in which are sunk deep wells; the old palace, or Alcazar, ruined by the French at the time of the invasion; the College, adorned with exquisite marble work, built by Cardinal Ximenes; saw the old Moorish walls and gateways, and the churches, and finally came to the celebrated Cathedral, ornamented with carvings of wood and stone, and lighted by exquisite painted windows.

It is about 400 feet in length by 200 in width, built in the Gothic style of architecture, surmounted by a tower 329 feet high, of great beauty, although not so beautiful as those of Burgos, and, like that Cathedral, is hidden by surrounding buildings. In one of the chapels we were shown the stone, surrounded by red jasper, on which the Virgin alighted when she appeared to San Idefonso, on this very spot, and, in return for his championship, clothed him with a chasuble of great splendor.

A very curious sight, too, is a statue of the Virgin, carved in *black* wood, seated on a silver throne, crowned with a tiara full of precious stones, and clothed in silk and brocade embroidered with gold and pearls. It is supposed to be 1,100 or 1,200 years old.

Toledo, on a rocky eminence, skirted by the "lordly Tagus," is the most pic-

Chapter VIII.—Toledo—La Mancha.

turesque city we saw in Spain. At present it is even more dead than Valladolid in appearance, and now but about 17,000 people live where once were courts of mighty monarchs, wealthy nobles, the celebrated Archbishops, who guided States and marshalled armies—familiar alike with court and camp—where 30,000 fighting men were mustered, and 10,000 hands were employed in its factories.

For 150 years Capital of Gothic Spain, 373 of Moorish Spain, and again the seat of the court of Charles V, now but a deserted town, with narrow, crooked streets, and interesting chiefly as a remnant of the past, "Ichabod" is written upon its gates.

Hence ifsued forth Don Roderick—to fight the invading Moor—in splendid state, attended by his noble cavaliers,—but hither returned he never. Here was born Perez de Vargas, that flower of chivalry, renowned in Spanish song. To-day the beggar sleeps in the sun, the water-carrier drones his monotonous song, and the glory of the past has faded.

After two or three days spent in Toledo, we set forth again for Cordova at six P. M. In a couple of hours we arrived at Castillejo, where we waited three more for a train. We talked with an old guard, to while away the time; and seeing him eat a sort of sugar-puff, soaked in a large glafs of water, tried it ourselves, but not with such great succefs as to induce us to repeat the experiment. Finally I borrowed from the bar-keeper (as we should call the man who sold water, wine, oranges and sugar,) a pack of cards. Spanish cards have no eight, nine or ten spots, nor are the face cards marked similarly to ours. Distinguishing them, however, as swords, cups, clubs and round things, it was pofsible to make a game of euchre, and so beguile the time until the train arrived.

We were told that we should reach Alcazar in an hour, but we fell asleep, and finally awaking, I found it was quarter to one, and there we were, flying along at a rate never before or since known in Spain, and only to be accounted for upon the

Chapter VIII.—Toledo—La Mancha.

theory that the locomotive had a sweetheart in Valencia, whom he was anxious to reach as soon as pofsible!

Painful surmises of our courier's having gone to sleep, as well as ourselves, flashed through our minds, and that instead of having changed cars at Alcazar, as we should have done, we were on our way to Valencia, while our baggage was *en route* for Cordova, (as happened to Commodore Mackenzie once upon a time—as told in his capital "Year in Spain,") and our large investment in diligence tickets was a failure. We had already begun to speculate on what we should do on arrival at Valencia—where we should be without a courier as well as baggage, for of course he would never appear before us again—when the train stopped, and the guard shouted "*Alcazar!*"

What was the matter with that place I do not know, but as it was a very cold night, I strongly suspect it had run down the road for twenty miles or so, in order to keep warm, and forgot to come back in time for the train.

Here we disembarked, and were shown into a huge room, where were perhaps an hundred men and women, dividing their attentions between coffee and sandwiches, and the endeavor to imitate the sounds at Babel, after the confusion of the builders' tongues. The nasal French, soft Italian, sonorous Spanish, and guttural German, were all heard, and close by us, from a form clothed in a capacious fur-lined coat, came the sound of sneezes ending with *ski*, which betrayed the Rufsian. Unwilling that America should be unrepresented in such a congrefs of nations, we contributed our share to the conversation, and attended to the coffee and sandwiches.

Being well warmed, we entered the cars again, awaking at five A. M. at Santa Cruz. Many drivers of rival diligences accosted us, upon whom we smiled blandly, answering them not again, while our excellent Manuel secured us our coupé, (or front compartment,) in the "Madrilena," a huge concern drawn by ten mules.

A woman presented hot chocolate, which,

Chapter VIII.—Toledo—La Mancha.

as the morning was frosty, was very refreshing, and we prepared for our long ride. Before leaving we received a number of calls from gentlemen resident in Santa Cruz, who addrefsed us with a series of remarks in Spanish, which, unfortunately, we were unable to understand. From their tone, and the frequent use of the words "*amor di Dios*," we concluded that they were either religious persons wishing to touch our hearts, or persons in impecunious circumstances, who desired to touch our pockets. We smiled benignantly upon them for some time, distributed a few coppers, and then, weary of their attentions, pulled up the windows of the coach. From their tone of voice as they turned away, we judged that the interview had not been altogether satisfactory to them, which we of course regretted.

"Crack went the whip, round went the wheels," and amid shouts and cries of the driver and whipper we were off. The whipper is an institution peculiar to this route, and, so far as I know, to this particular diligence, for I have never seen him described in any books. Drefsed in breeches, leggings and shirt, with a slouch hat and a gay waistband, he sits beside the driver, and makes it his businefs to see that the proper rate of speed is kept up. Should the stretch of level road be long, and the mules given to slow progrefs, or be they inclined to walk, or even trot slowly up hill, down jumps the vigilant whipper, runs to the front, and as each pair of animals pafses, he makes a long, limber stick bend over their backs, compelling them into a full gallop, and then picking up a few stones wherewith to pelt particular pets, he runs up again, swings himself lightly to the seat, and with his hand beating on his mouth, gives vent to a long howl of encouragement. As this ceremony is being continually performed, the whipper, though a very agile, active, spare young man, is changed with the mules every hour.

It was a lovely day for our ride. Unlike all other travelers who ever wrote concerning that route, we had no accidents, delays, or other matter, to complain of. The mules did not tangle up, nor stand on their heads; the diligence lost neither a wheel nor its balance; the road was in capital order; we had the best seats in the concern; and, with a good basket of cold chicken and partridge, and a bottle of Valdepeñas, we cared nothing for poor hotels by the way— in which, however, one can always procure good omelettes and bread, and excellent chocolate.

The road acrofs La Mancha is over a great sandy plain, with few villages of adobé houses, and a beggarly population. Corn and wine are the chief productions. Windmills tofs their long arms in the air, inviting attack from Don Quixote, and, as in the rest of Spain, few trees are to be seen.

The pafsage of the Sierra presents some interesting and wild mountain views; and here and there one sees parties of workmen, who are driving tunnels through the granite hills for the railroad to Cordova.

Although the ride was a pleasant one, and the day was fine, we were not sorry when, at ten o'clock in the evening, the diligence stopped before the door of a comfortable hotel in Cordova.

The postillion, who had ridden the foremost animal for seventeen consecutive hours, followed us into the hotel to claim his perquisite, and when we gave him half a dollar, retired fully satisfied.

Chapter IX.—*Cordova*.

GOOD sleep and an excellent breakfast caused us to forget the fatigues of our trip; and the next morning we first visited the Cathedral. The day was warm and sunny, presenting a great contrast to the climate of the northern elevated plains,—and as we paſsed along the clean streets, between rows of white houses with green balconies and blinds, and peeped through the gateways into the open courts, where orange and lemon trees were growing, laden with golden fruit, and the lofty palm towered above the plashing fountain,—we felt the charm of this beautiful Andalusia; and in answer to the question of our courier, how long we should stay in the city, my answer was instantaneous and earnest: "I don't feel now as if I should ever quit this place."

Entering the gate of the court of the Cathedral, we found ourselves in a grove of orange trees loaded with fruit, surrounding a fountain at which the faithful Moslem performed his ablutions before entering the sacred building—a practice which might be imitated by his Christian succefsors, greatly to their advantage.

Pafsing in through the principal entrance, we looked upon a building as singular in architecture as in beauty. With a low roof —seeming lower than it really is, by reason of the forest of marble pillars which support the double arches upon which it rests, and of great size,—it contrasted strongly with the Gothic Cathedrals we had lately visited. The effect is injured by the great choir and high altar erected in its centre; but, as we stood looking from one end through the pillars and arches, we remembered the days of its glory, when from fretted arches swung hundreds of lamps, the light of which

Chapter IX.—Cordova.

illumined the vast interior, and was reflected back from thousands of precious stones, while on the floor the turbaned Moslem bowed his head before the holy place where was kept the Koran, and we forgot the defect.

Nine hundred years ago, Cordova was the home of a million of people; the centre of learning and intelligence in the world; its rulers vied with oriental princes in luxury and state; the minarets of three hundred mosques rose in the air, while twice as many inns, and three times as many baths, were provided for the comfort of the inhabitants, and the crowds of strangers who resorted thither; and its chief mosque was inferior only to that of Damascus in size, and to the Caäba of Mecca in holinefs. Now—here and there—the quotations from the Koran may still be seen upon its walls; the pillars of marble, and jasper, and porphyry, brought from Nismes, and Narbonne, and Carthage, and Constantinople, still support the light arches; but the sixteen hundred lamps no longer are suspended from the roof; the brilliant coloring is hidden with whitewash; the organ peals and the censer swings within it; and the Moslem has left only the relics of his proud and elegant dominion. The grafs grows in the streets; learning and power have departed; and where a great multitude once gathered, but forty thousand now exist.

Not very far from the mosque, just out of one of the gates of the city, the Guadalquiver is spanned by a bridge, built by the Romans, guarded at the further end by a Moorish tower; while, at the other end, is the gate of the city erected by Ferdinand and Isabella,—presenting thus, hand in hand, relics of the three proudest of Spain's rulers.

In Cordova, as in Seville, the houses are built about square open courts, with covered arcades on each side, and fountains, orange and lemon trees, the cactus and other plants, and palm trees, in the centre. In the summer rods are put acrofs, over this open space, and the whole covered with an awning;

and the family, thus protected from the sun, having no rain to fear, bring down their furniture into the arcades, and spend their days in the open air.

After a short stay we went to Seville, the road running near the river, through fields hedged with the aloe and prickly pear, with here and there orchards of orange and olive trees, and now and then a palm. It is said that the first palm tree ever planted in Spain was brought there by one of the Moorish monarchs, who desired to thus keep green the memory of his beloved Damascus.

Chapter X.—*Seville.*

OF course, in Seville, as in Cordova, the first visit is to the Cathedral, a Gothic building, said to be the largest in the world, except St. Peter's in Rome, of which, however, I shall not attempt to give a labored description, as, like that, it has been so often described by others. At its side rises the Giralda—a tower 350 feet in height, built originally by the Moors, but changed at the summit and added to by the Spaniards subsequently. It is thirty-five feet square, and ascended, not by steps, but by a winding inclined plane inside, up which one could easily ride a horse. From the summit the view is very extended over the city and surrounding plain, through which

Chapter X.—Seville.

winds the Guadalquiver, sparkling in the sunlight. Near its top hangs a chime of twenty-five bells, being the same number as the churches in Seville.

On the summit of the tower is mounted an immense bronze figure of a woman holding a shield, said to weigh 9,000 pounds, so lightly poised as to turn with every breeze. It is singular enough that this weathercock bears the name of *Faith*.

Pafsing through the court, we enter the wondrous structure, and walk with reverence through the lofty naves, lighted with the "dim, religious light" that streams through the painted windows; stop before the tomb of St. Ferdinand, and muse of home as the eye rests upon the slab of marble that marks the grave of the son of Columbus.

But often must the traveler return in the morning to linger before the wonderful achievements of Murillo—"The Guardian Angel," and "St. Anthony of Padua." In the former, the angel, leading a little boy by the hand—the countenance of the angel filled with benignity and wisdom, that of the child exprefsive of innocence, franknefs and hope—fully justify the high praises bestowed upon the painting. The latter is thought to be one of Murillo's grandest works. The infant Jesus, in the midst of cherubs, angels, and light, descends to blefs his faithful follower in answer to his prayers. The Duke of Wellington is said to have offered to cover the picture, which is very large, with gold pieces, as the price for its purchase, but the chapter refused to sell.

In the Hospital, *La Caridad*, we saw two other celebrated works of this great master —one called "The Thirst"—*La Sed*— representing "Moses Striking the Rock," from which gushes the water eagerly caught by the famished multitude,—the other, "The Miracle of the Loaves and the Fishes." Here formerly hung also "Santa Isabella," washing the sores of a beggar-boy's head—a picture remarkable alike for the beauty of Isabella and her attendants, and the accurate loathsomenefs of the sufferers; but after Marshal Soult had carried it to Paris, and it had been restored, it remained in Madrid, instead of being returned to its original position, for which the subject is peculiarly suited.

Two of the most interesting sights in Seville are the *Casa Pilata*, or House of Pilate, and the *Alcazar*.

The former, a curious mixture of Moorish and Gothic architecture, is so called because it has a room said to resemble in every particular a portion of the house of Pilate of Judea, and a stone pillar is said to be the *fac simile* of that at which Christ was scourged.

The latter was formerly the Moorish palace, added to and enlarged by the various rulers of Spain; restored to its ancient style of ornamentation and splendor, it is now kept as one of the royal palaces.

In no place in Spain did I experience the same sense of the physical luxury that the Moors delighted in. Standing on the cool marble floor, in a room of which the walls are richly adorned with delicate tracery of stucco, colored with gold, and red, and blue, and green,—looking through a long vista of gorgeous rooms—through arches fretted with seeming lace-work, with the sun pouring his golden light in at the windows—while the cool breezes are laden with the fragrance of tropical flowers and the rich scent of orange blofsoms, and the song of birds and the plash of fountains fall upon the ear—one can not help wishing for a day to spend with the learned, elegant and luxurious Moor.

"It is impofsible," says Irving, "to travel about Andalusia, and not imbibe a kind feeling for those Moors. They deserved this beautiful country. They won it bravely; they enjoyed it generously and kindly. No lover ever delighted more to cherish and adorn a mistrefs, to heighten and illustrate her charms, and to vindicate and defend her against all the world, than did the Moors to embellish, elevate and enrich their beloved Spain. Everywhere I met traces of their sagacity, courage, urbanity, high poetical feeling, and elegant taste. The noblest institutions in this part of Spain, the best inventions for comfort-

Chapter X.—Seville.

able and agreeable living, and all those habitudes and customs which throw a peculiar and oriental charm over the Andalusian mode of living, may be traced to the Moors. Whenever I enter these beautiful marble patios, set out with shrubs and flowers, refreshed by fountains, sheltered with awnings from the sun; where the air is cool at noonday, the ear delighted in sultry summer by the sound of falling water; where, in a word, a little paradise is shut up within the walls of home; I think on the poor Moors, the inventors of all these delights. I am at times almost ready to join in sentiment with a worthy friend and countryman whom I met in Malaga, who swears the Moors are the only people that ever deserved the country, and prays to heaven they may come over from Africa and conquer it again."

I think that friend a most sensible person, and if they should return with the keys to their dwellings, which they have handed down from generation to generation, to take pofsefsion and dwell there, and again make the fertile soil bring forth its fruit by their patient toil, and restore the magnificence of the olden time, I, for one, would bid them God speed!

From such buildings as the Alcazar, to go to the Cannon Foundry, and the Tobacco Factory, where 5,000 women are employed, and where the stranger must endure the ordeal of 5,000 tongues and 10,000 bright inquisitive eyes, is like awaking from a delicious reverie after reading the "Arabian Nights," to find oneself in the reality of a political meeting.

An intermediate step is the Museum, where are collected several works of Murillo and a number by other Spanish artists of note. Zurbaran has one representing a dozen or so of monks, with white robes and red caps, seated at a table on a fast-day, whereon are dishes laden with smoking meats and such carnal luxuries. Enters unto them the prior of the convent, with stern visage, and the surprised sinners are filled with the empty wind of consternation, instead of the anticipated forbidden flesh.

Chapter X.—Seville.

The attitudes and exprefsion of the countenances are capital.

One of the principal streets in Seville, where ladies go shopping—for as babies in all countries cry in the same language, so do women in all countries alike delight in shopping—has rods extended acrofs from the roofs of the houses, over which in summer an awning is drawn, keeping the walk—for no carriages are allowed to enter—clean and cool—a fashion to be envied in our heated terms.

As we were riding along in the city one day, we had a rather exciting opportunity to see one of the favorite amusements in Seville. The street was not wide enough to turn in, and straight before and trotting towards us was a wild bull, with lofty head and fiery eye, followed by a crowd of screaming boys and men. If he had taken a fancy to pay attention to our horses, we should have had a private bull-fight that we did not relish the prospect of, the advantage being all on the bull's side. But he pafsed by and made for an old woman, whose gaily covered cloak attracted his attention. She, called to a sense of her situation by the clamor of the crowd, rushed into an open doorway and escaped, and the animal proceeded on his way, monarch of the street.

The city itself lies on the left bank of the Guadalquiver, which winds around its walls, which are about five miles in circumference, with sixty-six towers and fifteen gates.

A prosperous trading seat under the Phœnicians; favored by the Romans; erected into the capital of Bœtica by Julius Cæsar; the court of the Gothic monarchs for fifty years; the most important city in Spain, after Cordova, under the Moors; famous for its silks and other fabrics, its schools and universities, and its extensive trade,—it was taken by Ferdinand, A. D. 1248, and its population of 400,000 Moors, Jews, and Arabs, driven without its walls.

"It was the beloved city of the Moslem —the gold and lace tent of the sensual Eastern—who planted it on the banks of the Guadalquiver, to dream life away amid the enchantments of refined taste, which he lavished his gold and genius to adorn, and his blood to defend and fortify. Here once, in the evening twilight, the muezzin's monotonous cry rang through the still air from the rosy towers of the Giralda, calling myriads of Moslems to prayer. The halls of the Alcazar, all glittering with gold and vivid colors, bathed in an ocean of light, were thronged with crowds of courtiers, garbed in long flowing robes, haughty warriors in floating burnooses, grey-bearded Alfaquirs, and obsequious ambafsadors from the courts of Castile, Arragon, Genoa, and other States. Its voluptuous harems extended amidst palm and orange groves to the river's banks, where black-eyed houris whiled their listlefs hours away, gazing on the Guadalquiver, where rocked on its crystal bosom heavily-laden, white-sailed feluccas, bearing the commerce of the world. Its bazaars were then full of the richest silks, in the manufacture of which upwards of two hundred thousand persons were employed. Its schools — rivals in learning of those at Cordova and Grenada —were frequented by the very Castilian and Arragonese princes, whose fathers envied the magnificence of this court and dreaded the valor of its armies. * * * Not only a city of pleasures and the repository of arts, but the centre, with Cordova, of European civilization."

Over one of its gates is inscribed the following couplet:

> "Condidit Alcides—renovavit Julius urbem,
> Restituit Christo Fernandus tertius heros."

And the Sevillians declare that he who hath not seen Seville, hath not seen a wonder.

> "Quien no ha visto Sevilla,
> No ha visto maravilla."

And certainly no book can give one a clear idea of the charms of the cities of Andalusia; they must be seen in order to be appreciated.

At the siege of the city, by Ferdinand, occurred the gallant act of Don Garcia Perez de Vargas, who rode, as told by Lockhart in his ballads, through a band of

Chapter X.—Seville.

seven Moors, and then having dropped his scarf, rode back again alone for it, his enemies each time fearing to attack a knight of such renown.

We had pleasant rooms at the *Hotel de Paris*, looking out upon an open space, through which the cavalry marched every day to the music of the "barbarous horn;" and when tired with rambling about, we would sit by the window, looking out upon the little booth below—where water, lemonade, almond-water, and similar beverages, were sold to thirsty Spaniards—and watch the paſsers-by,—now a couple of priests, with long black gowns, and felt hats, with wide rims rolled up at the side, and projecting half a yard in front and rear—now a woman, with gloſsy black hair and graceful mantilla—now a water-carrier, with his jar upon his head, crying his "*acqua frisca;*" and here and there a beggar—such as Murillo would have loved to put upon the canvaſs—with sun-browned skin, and countenance expreſsive of content with rags.

When tired of these amusements, and

of eating oranges freshly pulled from the blofsom-covered tree, it was delightful to turn to the pages of Prescott and Irving, and bring the past vividly to mind.

One morning I started out to see the *Barber of Seville.* His house I found, but *Figaro* is no longer *qui* nor *là;* but a sober carpenter occupies his premises. Not fancying being shaved with a plane, I returned to the hotel.

It was delightful at Seville, with its grand Cathedral and gorgeous palace, its clean streets, pictures, balconied houses, and walks through groves of orange trees, whose golden fruit peeped from the dark green foliage, while the blofsoms perfumed the air; but time was precious, and reluctantly we left for Cadiz.

CHAPTER XI.—*Cadiz—Gibraltar.*

THE hotels of Cadiz are all poor, says Harper's Handbook, and so far as my experience goes, it leads me to credit that afsertion. Certainly the hotel was poor in comparison with those of New York and Philadelphia, the quiet inns of England, or the luxurious palaces of Switzerland; but compared with those of Burgos and Valladolid, our hotel was a luxurious abode. It was cold in the evenings certainly, and when tired of shivering in shawls and overcoats, we inhaled headaches from the *brazero*, and were not in a frame of mind to praise the hotel very highly. But the bed was clean, the table fair, and the sherry cheap and exceedingly dry.

We intended to spend but a day in Cadiz; but in Spain things are never done as in other countries, and so it happened that every day we walked down the street, and read one or more advertisements of veſsels to sail on the morrow posted on the walls, and comforting ourselves with hope, proceeded to the *Alameda*, where we walked up and down the long gravelled promenade, looking out upon the sparkling sea, or up at the two tall palms which stand like sentinels near the church; or sat in the sun in the open square, eating bananas, in contemplative mood; or rambled by the city walls, watching the fishermen, and enjoying the lovelineſs of the beautiful bay. And these amusements, except that of a cigar and a New York paper at the Consul's office, of a morning, were about all that Cadiz had to offer.

There is no sight-seeing to be done, which perhaps is rather a relief than otherwise; and in spite of Byron, and travelers in general, I could not rouse any enthusiasm whatever over the beauty of the ladies.

Chapter XI.—Cadiz—Gibraltar.

They walk well, and show now and then a dainty foot and ankle, but English and Germans are not good judges of such matters. The English, who are born with umbrellas, rave over the skies of any country where it does not rain every day, and neither in all England nor Germany, are there so many pretty women as in New York City. But an American, who has lived among beautiful women all his life, is more critical. One whose knowledge of art is confined to the photographic gallery of a small town, will vastly admire a painting which he who is accustomed to the treasures of Florence and of Rome, will pafs by without a second glance.

One morning, strolling into a church which offered no particular architectural attraction, I noticed one of the Cadiz ladies on her knees before the altar. A young man pafsing through a side aisle called to her, and some pleasant remarks pafsed between them, when he proceeded on his way, and she took up her prayers again. A few such sights as this will cause one to ask himself, whether the prohibition of all conversation between men and women, posted up in large letters on the walls of the Cathedral at Malaga, under the penalty of a *fine of two dollars and excommunication*, is altogether needlefs.

One fine morning we were to start for Xerez, under the care of our obliging Consul, but he not being able to be absent long enough for that trip, we went to Puerto Santa Maria, to see the wine-cellars there. An Englishman, acting as American Vice-Consul, received us very politely, and was our guide for the morning. His name was Crusoe, and he was, he averred, a lineal descendant of the famous Robinson. He himself had a small wine-house, which we examined; but the chief interest of the trip was centered in one—the name of the owner of which I do not remember—containing 8,000 casks. These wine-houses, or *bodegas* as they are called, are on the surface of the ground, instead of being below it; but being large, lofty and dark, are cool and pleasant. We tasted many varieties of wine, and listened to a long account of the manufacture of the wine, through all the stages; but I may be excused from attempting to give a long recital of it, with my recollection impaired by the time that has elapsed since then. Suffice it to say, it was very interesting, and, with delicate Manzanilla and Amontillado, by no means dry.

On the way home we occupied the same car with a muscular mifsionary from Africa, who was taking Cadiz *en route* for England, whose tongue being loosed, gave us some wonderful stories of boar hunting, and explained how much more safe it was to knock down Jews than Moors. The gentle mifsionary was also returning from a visit to the *bodegas*, and was seemingly much elated by what he had seen.

At last, one afternoon, we were notified that a boat would certainly start that evening for Gibraltar precisely at nine o'clock, and that we must be on board before dark. So hastening dinner, we got together our traps, and set out. In a few minutes we were rowed to the vefsel, and having secured a state-room, retired early, expecting to wake at Gibraltar. But we did not yet understand Spanish ways. It was four in the morning before we started, and we reached Gibraltar about noon.

In a few minutes we were pulled along shore by some Spanish boatmen, and our baggage followed us to the Custom-House, where, for the first time in Spain, my pafsport was demanded by a tall, awkward soldier, with a tight, red jacket, little skull cap, fastened to the side of his head, and a short rattan. Producing this, examination of baggage was waived, and I received a permit to remain three days in the town, which, however, I did not take the trouble afterward to have renewed. On the landing was gathered the most motley crowd I ever saw—turbaned Turks and Moors, red-capped Greeks, English soldiers and sailors, dirty Italians, and Spaniards, and Jews, with a very Babel of sounds.

Moors are plentiful at Gibraltar—some with long robe and turban, but the great majority clothed in a simple garment like a

Chapter XI.—Cadiz—Gibraltar.

shirt of dirty white, leaving the arms and legs below the knee bare, skull cap on the head, and heelleſs slippers on their feet. The most remarkable thing about them is their walk. Large and well made, they have an erectneſs of figure and elasticity of step, which always commanded my admiration.

We found a very comfortable sitting-room, with two most remarkable pieces of furniture—a piano and a fire-place—at the King's Arms Hotel, and a bed-room, which, though of the plainest, was most comfortable; and, of course, at an English hotel, plenty of water, and the invigorating bleſsing of Baſs, whom a Cambridge student is said to have once pronounced the greatest benefactor of mankind.

Having letters to the Governor-General, and to Col. B., commanding an infantry regiment there, I took a hansom—just think of a hansom in Spain—and delivered them. Their receipt was followed by invitations to lunch and dinner, and many kind attentions on the part of Col. B., who also entertained us at his quarters, and took us all over the rock.

The rock rises abruptly from the sea on the eastern side, sloping down to Europa Point at the southern end, with an almost perpendicular face towards Spain. The slope on the western side is gradual, affording good roads and walks, while at the foot of the descent lie a few acres of almost level ground, whereon are situated the gardens and town.

The town itself is old, dirty, and uninteresting; but the gardens, with groves of trees and shrubbery, lawns, and gravelled walks lined with geranium, cacti, and other flowers, are very beautiful, and afforded us many hours of pleasure. Contiguous to the gardens is a large, open, gravelled space, where the garrison is drilled, affording quite a brilliant scene in the mornings. Toward the southern end of the rock are the barracks and officers' quarters—some of the latter having neat little cottages, with gardens, and a profusion of flowers.

One morning, after walking over to

Col. B.'s quarters, a couple of miles from the hotel, and lunching with him, we walked to Europa Point, where he showed us the triple line of fortifications, each higher than that in front of it, that defend the southern approaches, and then wound round by a road to the eastern side. At some distance up the side of the rock is a cave, to which entrance is now forbidden, on account of the loſs of a couple of exploring soldiers in it some time since. The inhabitants of the rock believe that there is a great hole in it extending down into the sea. Reaching about the middle of the eastern side, the road ends, and we mounted stone steps, partly natural and partly artificial, to the summit, and after walking a few minutes longer, arrived at the highest point—1,430 feet above the sea —where is the signal station. A small house stands there, to accommodate the signal-master and his family, who, by request of the Colonel, brought us "*shandygaff*," a drink made by mixing one bottle of pale ale with two of ginger-beer, and one which we found very refreshing after our tramp. There were formerly many monkeys living on the rock, but they have all disappeared except seven, which are forbidden to be molested, and of the appearance of each of which a record is kept by the signal-master.

Three great guns are mounted there, pointing over the town, of which one is fired in the morning, one in the evening, after which all ingrefs and egrefs beyond the lines are forbidden, and a third at noon. When it is desired to give an alarm, as in case of fire or mutiny, the three are fired in rapid succefsion.

Somewhat fatigued with climbing up the mountain, we sat sipping our *shandygaff*, and enjoying the magnificent prospect. To the east was the blue Mediterranean, on whose shores were raised the cities, and on whose bosom sailed the argosies of the nations of the dim past, now covered with the white sails of western bound vefsels, detained by contrary winds. To the south stretched Africa, land of the

Chapter XI.—Cadiz—Gibraltar.

unknown. Before us rose the twin pillars of Hercules, and near by lay Tangier, from which embarked the Moslem on his conquering mifsion. On the east, Tarifa, where he landed, shone white in the sun; a little further stood the lighthouse of Cape Trafalgar, off the shore of which Nelson won his famous victory; and beyond rolled the waters of the turbulent Atlantic, over which fancy easily wafted us to the society of friends and home. To the north lay the plains and mountains of Spain, the white village of San Roque, a few miles distant, the dark shadows of the cork wood, and, between us and them, the neutral ground, on the respective borders of which paced the sentinels of either country.

Not far southward from where we sat, was an old ruin, which we visited, of a tower built long ago by Governor O'Hara, with the idea that from its summit, with a proper glafs, one could see over the intervening hills, and command a view of the Bay of Cadiz. As might be supposed, it was labor lost.

Descending the western side of the rock, sometimes by winding walks, and again by long flights of steps, which shortened the distance, we were overtaken by a shower, and hastened to our hotel, arriving just in time for an English roast of beef, which, after over five hours' constant walking, we were not sorry to see.

One of the chief curiosities of the rock consists in its galleries, or tunnels, cut into the northern end. These are paſsages of several feet in width, and of an average of eight or ten feet in height, from which, at intervals, open chambers of considerable size, their windows forming port-holes, through which cannon keep watch upon all the Spanish frontier. There are several of these galleries extending to the eastern side of the rock.

This great natural fortreſs is mounted with seven hundred guns, mostly of the Armstrong pattern, and furnished with cisterns of water, and magazines of ammunition and provisions, hollowed out of the rock, sufficient to enable a proper garrison to resist a five years' siege.

The weather, while we were there, in March, was most delightful, not too warm for exercise, nor too cool for open windows, and the gardens were filled with flowers.

Our Consul, Mr. S.—to whom, as to his accomplished wife, we were indebted for many kind attentions, and for keeping us *au courant* with American news—has a farm a few miles from Gibraltar, to which we drove one morning, returning laden with beautiful flowers.

Chapter XII.—*Malaga.*

WE had intended to remain but two or three days in Gibraltar, but there, as in Cadiz, boats were uncertain, and it was a week before we departed.

At five o'clock, on a bright, warm morning, we were rowed out to a small steamer lying in the bay, bound for Malaga. Climbing on board, we found an English peer—a young English gentleman whom we afterward learned to call Viscount—and his tutor, and a couple of Spanish girls, in black dreſses, black mantillas, black eyes, and black hair, carefully arranged. Afterward appeared a tall Spaniard, with a rich cloak, bordered within with maroon-colored velvet, and a dirty old fellow, who

Chapter XII.—Malaga.

turned out to be one of the rich merchants of Malaga.

The boat was small, with one tiny cabin below deck, and seats along the sides of the deck where all sat down. In an hour or two we started. We sailed round the great rock, the shadow of which lay resting on the sea, through the straits, and into the blue waters of the Mediterranean. The sea was as smooth as glafs, and as we coasted along, we watched the changing shores, and the half-naked boatmen busy on the water.

About nine o'clock, feeling the want of breakfast, I went below, and found two or three sitting at the table; and inquiring what I could have for breakfast, was answered: "Any thing you wish, Señor." "Any chicken?" "No chicken, Señor; but any thing else." "Any ham?" "No ham, Señor; but any thing else Señor wishes." After a variety of questions, I learned that "any thing" meant eggs, bread without butter, vile coffee without milk, and beer. I ordered some eggs and bread, and we were falling into travelers' conversation, when we were startled by a loud "Aha! Aha!" at the door. Looking round, we perceived the dirty old merchant, who, coming in, pafsed on to a vacant place at the head of the table, stopping to pat the young viscount on the head, much to the latter's disgust. Having ordered some eggs and bread, he pulled from his trowsers' pocket a newspaper parcel, which being unrolled proved to contain a thick sausage. Laying it on his plate, and gazing on it fondly, he gave vent to another loud "Aha!" Then slicing off some pieces with his knife, he shoved them upon the plate of his neighbor, who protested against it. But not understanding that any one would not really like his sausage, he only smiled, and did the same good office for his neighbor on the other side. Fearing his kindnefs might reach me, I pushed away my plate. Soon he sliced up the remainder —about a pound—on his own plate, and once again vented his satisfaction in a resonant "Aha!"

I left the room and came on deck. For

Chapter XII.—Malaga.

a time the scene was delightful, but about noon the wind began to blow, the sea to rise, and soon we were in the midst of one of those southern gales for which the Mediterranean is famous—sinking now so that we could only see the spars of a sailing vefsel at a little distance, and then, mounting to the top of a wave, having a view of the whole craft. It was disturbing, to say the least of it, and every one finally paid unwilling tribute to Neptune, the Spaniard alone excepted. Sitting near the edge of the deck, he extended his arms about the miserable Spanish girls, encouraging them, when any more violent paroxysms occurred, with the philosophical remark that it was a capital thing for them; in the meantime addrefsing them tenderly as his dearest and most beautiful, much to the amusement of all who were not too sick to watch him. The sausage-man had disappeared, and I did not see him until we had anchored in the Bay of Malaga, when, descending to the cabin for my bag and umbrella, I saw the old fellow stretched upon a sofa, neither saying, looking nor thinking "Aha!" As I turned to go out, he made an effort to rise, but the vessel giving another roll, he fell again to work, and I saw him no more. Probably, as the poet says, "If he hasn't got up, he lies there still."

A good hotel, a good glass of sherry, a hot bath, and a good dinner, soon set all right again. We met some Bostonians, who were very pleasant people, and if it had not been for an opera singer, who was screeching her loudest in the next room, until the small hours, greatly to the gratification of a party who were loudly applauding, we should have enjoyed our first night in Malaga very much.

The city presents a fine appearance from the sea, and is a large town of some 95,000 inhabitants, chiefly occupied with winegrowing and trade. Screened by the northern hills from cold winds, and open on the sea to the warm eastern and southern breezes, it is a favorite winter resort for invalids. About the fourteenth century the climate was much more moist, owing

Chapter XII.—Malaga.

to the thick forests with which the hills were clothed; but during the wars waged against the Moors, these were cut down, and if it were not for the abundant dews, vegetation would disappear, and the coast become a barren desert.

The harbor is deep and capacious enough to accommodate over four hundred ships; and wines, raisins, figs, lemons, oranges, almonds, and other fruits, are largely exported. The dry Malaga wine is manufactured in great quantities, and the exquisite, but very sweet, "*Lagrimas*," or "tears," made from the first juice of the grape without prefsure, is celebrated.

There is said to gather pleasant society at Malaga; there is a promenade along the sea shore, a library, and conveniences of correspondence, but few objects of interest. The Cathedral is chiefly attractive for its fine marbles, taken from the native mountains, and one or two paintings by Alonso Cano; and the public fountain, with little jets of water spouting from the mouths of toads, ducks, snakes, etc., is more curious than beautiful.

The reader of Irving's "Granada" will find a charm of historical reminiscence hanging about the city and its environs, but the general traveler will find little to detain him.

The regular diligence for Granada starts in the evening, compelling the traveler to lose the fine scenery of the route, while the mail-stage, which has two spare seats only, leaves just before daylight. We decided therefore to send our courier forward with the baggage in the evening, and follow ourselves the next morning. So at half-past two we were called, and set forth for the starting place of the mail-diligence. Traversing various streets, dimly lighted by straggling lamps, we reached a court as dark as midnight, in which, feeling about, we found a seat. In an hour more the horses were hitched, and taking our places, we rattled out of the town.

Our course stretched nearly due north to Loja, over the mountains, and for some hours we enjoyed most beautiful mountain scenery. An hour or so after leaving

Chapter XII.—Malaga.

Malaga, one obtains a superb view of the city and surrounding country, and the blue sea beyond; and afterwards, as he winds along between the lofty peaks of granite and marble, with here and there a verdant valley, or a peak covered with snow, he will not regret his early start instead of the night ride. The air was sharp when we started, and after a few hours' ride, we had reason to praise our own forethought in bringing along a well filled basket and bottle.

At Loja we entered upon the famed Vega —or plain—of Granada, stretching some thirty miles in length by about twenty-five in breadth, watered by the Douro, and the Xenil and its tributaries, intersected with canals, dug for purposes of irrigation by the Moors, and rich in beauty and fertility.

About five o'clock we arrived in Granada, and wearied with the journey, sought water, food and rest.

Chapter XIII.

Granada—Madrid—Saragofsa—Barcelona.

IN the town there is little of interest except the Cathedral, of considerable dimensions, enriched with beautiful Spanish marbles. It is called the *Cathedral of Ave Maria,* and the story of the name is as follows:

When Ferdinand and Isabella were besieging Granada, Count de Pulgar, a knight of great prowefs and audacity, fired with zeal to revenge the daring outrage of a Moorish warrior, who, sallying forth, had thrown his javelin so that it quivered in the ground hard by the tent of the Spanish sovereigns, gathered together a small band of cavaliers of kindred spirit, and riding to

Chapter XIII.—Granada, &c.

an ill-defended gate, on a dark night, attacked and overpowered the guard there stationed. Leaving his companions to continue the fight, and keep the gate, he put spurs to his horse, galloped to the mosque in the centre of the city, and nailed to its door with his dagger a placard bearing the words "Ave Maria." Then he rode back again, and, rejoining his companions, returned to the Spanish camp. There was great indignation of the Moors, and corresponding joy among the Spaniards, when the exploit became known, and afterwards, when the city was taken, the mosque was converted into a Cathedral—on the site of which the present Cathedral stands—and named the Church of Ave Maria.

On the high altar of the Royal Chapel is a curious bas-relief, representing the surrender of the city by Boabdil; but the most interesting objects are the tombs of Ferdinand and Isabella, of most delicately wrought alabaster, surmounted by full-length figures, of which the attitude and exprefsion are most admirable.

Before its capture, "the city was surrounded," says Irving in his Granada, "by high walls, three leagues in circuit, furnished with twelve gates and a thousand and thirty towers. Its elevation above the sea, and the neighborhood of the Sierra Nevada, crowned with perpetual snows, tempered the fervid rays of summer; so that while other cities were panting with the sultry and stifling heat of the dog-days, the most salubrious breezes played through the marble halls of Granada."

On one of the hills, twenty-six hundred and ninety feet long, and seven hundred and thirty broad, in its widest part, surrounded with lofty walls and towers, stands the famous *Alhambra*.

Entering the gate, and ascending by a winding road through groves that are the homes of hundreds of nightingales, by the side of a stream of crystal water, which, as well as the fountains, are furnished by canals from the snows of the mountains, we soon arrived at the Alhambra proper, or royal palace.

This formerly was about four hundred feet in length, by two hundred in breadth, but portions of it have been torn away for various purposes; and in one part is an unfinished palace commenced by Charles the Fifth. The *Hall of the Ambafsadors*, however, thirty-seven feet square, and seventy-five in height, overlooking the Douro; the *Court of the Lions*, with its beautiful fountain, guarded by twelve lions little resembling the live animal, surrounded by arcades supported by pillars of marble and alabaster, and covered with exquisite designs, and Arabic inscriptions in stucco; the *Hall of the Abencerrages*, where they are said to have been murdered, and other rooms, are still remaining, and are of wondrous beauty, although their ancient splendor of gold and brilliant colors has been obscured by whitewash. At present, however, workmen are busy restoring the rooms to their original condition.

The appearance of these celebrated halls has been rendered too familiar by other and more able writers to warrant me in attempting the task. Suffice it to say, that no description can do them justice, or repay one who is able to do so, for not seeing them for himself, and enjoying, on the spot, the charming descriptions and legends of Irving and other accomplished writers.

As we stood upon one of the towers, on which was a slab recording the date of the capture, by Ferdinand and Isabella, in 1492, at our feet lay the city and the winding stream; far down as the eye could reach, extended the verdant Vega, to the left rose the hill where the departing Boabdil took his last look upon his beloved city, and behind, seemingly so near that one could walk to them in half an hour, rose the snow-covered summits of the Sierra. I remember no view in Europe, which, for beauty and variety, mingled with historic and poetical afsociation, can equal it. Profefsor Longfellow somewhere exprefses a doubt whether Heidelberg or the Alhambra be the finest ruin, but to me the latter is very much the more interesting and beautiful.

Chapter XIII.—Granada, &c.

On the breast of the hill above the Alhambra is the palace of the *Generalife*, embowered in flowers and trees, and forming as fine a summer retreat as one could wish; but the owner has never visited it, and it merely serves as a home for the old guardian, and an object of interest to the traveler.

Granada was the last remaining kingdom of the Moors, after eight hundred years of power. In it were gathered all the learning, luxury and splendor of the race, and while they clung to it with all the ardor of their natures, they were long compelled to defend it with the sword. But at last, after a long siege, during which deeds of desperate valor were performed on both sides, Boabdil was compelled to surrender his last stronghold, and present to the conquerors the golden keys of the city.

"There was crying in Granada, when the sun was going down,
Some calling on the Trinity, some calling on Mahoun;
Here pafsed away the Koran, there in the Crofs was borne,
And here was heard the Christian bell, and there the Moorish horn.

"*Te Deum Laudamus*" was up the Alcala sung;
Down from the Alhamra's minarets were all the crescents flung;
The arms thereon of Arragon they with Castile's display;
One king comes in, in triumph, one weeping goes away."

Cui bono? There was the triumph of the Christian King over the infidel, but the fruits have been allowed to wither and decay, and in the contrast of the ignorant and degraded population of the present day with the intelligent and laborious inhabitants who were dispersed, one can read that the glory has turned into ashes in the victors' grasp, and one more witnefs testifies to the fact that the true triumphs of Christianity are to be sought, not by means of the cannon nor the sword, but through the gentler and surer influences of reason, affection and example.

"From Granada to Madrid, by diligence, twenty-two hours, and by rail ten," says my note-book. And a long and wearisome journey it was, for a great part of the way over the same road we had come *en ronte* for Cordova. The change from the charming country of Andalusia to the plains of

La Mancha, and the cold air of Madrid, was not altogether pleasant. Arriving at Santa Cruz about eight in the morning, we had to wait some four hours for a train. We secured a room to lie down in, to which we mounted by a ladder. Through the cracks of the floor was visible the table spread below, and the conversation was, as it were, in the same room with us. The floor of the first story was literally the ground floor, being of hard-beaten earth. It was, however, the best accommodation the town afforded, and we were glad to get a little rest.

We had not been there half an hour before half a dozen men and boys were playing cards in front of the house, with a board for a table, staking copper or silver coins, according to the ability of the owners. The pafsion for gambling is universal in Spain, and there is hardly a person who does not have a chance in one of the lotteries, which, a Spaniard told me one day, were "the only fair things carried on by the Government."

Arriving at Madrid in the evening, we found our former rooms vacant, and for two or three days enjoyed the comforts of a good hotel, and the pleasure of the society of our friends.

From Madrid to Saragofsa is only two hundred and fifteen miles, but the exprefs train was thirteen hours in reaching it. Enough of daylight remained for a walk about the town, to see its Square and Leaning Tower, and general characteristics; and in the evening we recalled its military renown and the fame of the Maid of Saragofsa, who performed such wonders in its defense, and is rendered immortal by Byron in his "Childe Harold." The city is the resort of the pious for the purpose of worship at the "*Pillar of the Virgin*"—a jasper pillar on which she is said to have alighted from heaven; and crowds of people resort thither on the 12th of October. There are about 70,000 inhabitants, but the city is not very interesting except to the artist, so we proceeded the next day about the same distance, at the same rate of speed, to Barcelona, which derives its name from Barca, father of Hannibal.

Favorably situated in regard to climate, and the chief shipping port of Spain, it ranks first among the commercial cities, and is second only to Madrid in population —having about 184,000 inhabitants. The streets are wide, clean, and well paved; the public walk—here called the *Rambla*—is lined with trees, and is a favorite resort of both sexes; and the Opera-House, which, however, was closed when we were there, is said to be larger than either that at Milan or Naples. It is the only city in Spain which bears evidence of commercial prosperity, and the bustling, busy life that prevails in commercial cities of other countries. Wide avenues, lined with stately buildings, are rapidly extending, and the population seem to have cast off the cloak of the past, which so closely enwraps the Spanish character, and to have learned to share with the rest of the world in the activity of the present.

The country through which we pafsed,

coming from Madrid, is very attractive, with wild and rugged mountains, quaint villages, old castles, dark olive orchards, and beautiful and fertile valleys. The people are tall and fine looking, and have an air of sturdy independence that one acquainted with their history might expect to find.

Chapter XIV.—*Leaving Spain.*

AFTER a short stay in Barcelona, we proceeded by rail northward, to Gerona, where we bade good-bye to Manuel, and took the diligence for Perpignan. Soon after starting it began to rain, for the first time since we left Bayonne, and soon fell in torrents. When we reached Boscara, about twenty miles on the way, at the beginning of the mountains, the diligence stopped, and the conductor, opening our door, said, touching his hat, "*Il faut coucher ici, Monsieur.*" Sleep there! Why should we not go on? The rain had melted the snow on the mountains, and the stream before us in the valley, usually fordable, was now a raging torrent, and still rising. What was to be done? There were no inns fit to stay in, and we might remain there—as we in fact did—twenty-four hours, and it rained harder than ever. Slipping a gold piece into the conductor's hand, I begged him to see what he could do for us, when he recollected a peasant's house hard by, where he thought we might pofsibly be accommodated. He went to ascertain, and presently returned, saying that the woman wanted to see us first. Luckily, the personal inspection proved favorable to our interests, and the good man consenting, we were taken to the best room in the second story. A very nice room it was, too—very plain, and simply furnished, and floored with brick, but as neat and clean as pofsible.

Soon came the question what we would like to eat, and by dint of help from our French-speaking conductor, who came to our afsistance, we had a capital meal of cutlets and delicious salad—which none know so well as Spaniards how to prepare —bread, and wine. After dinner we pro-

Chapter XIV.—Leaving Spain.

ceeded to the kitchen, where the hostefs was cooking dinner for her husband, and his son and workmen, who were all busy finishing an addition to the house. It was a veritable *olla podrida*—such as we had heard of, but never tasted.

Over a small fire of little faggots, in the corner of the kitchen, hung a pot, into which were put water, cabbage, vermicelli, potatoes, bread, salt, an onion and a bit of garlic, and a piece of meat. When the stew was ready, they all came in and seated themselves round the table, in the centre of which stood a capacious dish filled with the savory mefs. Each had a soup-plate and spoon, and proceeded to help himself to the *olla*, as well as to large slices of bread from the loaf. In the dish of the proprietor and his wife and son, a thicker stew of potatoes and meat was poured. Wine was upon the table, in a glafs vefsel of conical form, with a small spout at the side, shaped almost exactly like a tin oil-can. There was nothing to drink out of, however, and I was curious to see how the operation would be conducted. We were invited to sit down, and having a curiosity to taste the *olla*, we did so. It was simply a very nice thick soup, with a slight flavor of garlic, to which, however, one soon becomes accustomed when traveling in Spain. Presently our host lifted the wine jar, and raised it towards his mouth, but instead of putting it to his lips, he inclined his head a little backward, and holding it about four or five inches from and above him, let a stream flow dextrously down his throat. Each followed in turn, and spurred with emulation, I tried the experiment, succeeding in getting some into my mouth, and more upon my chin and shirt, much to their amusement.

In the morning, when we rose, a cup of hot chocolate was ready for us, and afterwards a breakfast much like the dinner of the day before. The hostefs, whose heart we seemed to have won, took us into her private room, and showed us their treasures —a large image of the Virgin, richly drefsed, and kept in a sort of niche made for the

Chapter XIV.—Leaving Spain.

purpose, and two large books. These, she said, with great pride, their son could read, although neither she nor her husband could either read or write. During the course of conversation, which was carried on chiefly by signs, pointing to her husband with one hand, she said, "Gerona;" then to herself with the other, said, "Valencia;" then placing her two forefingers together, said, "Barcelona;" all of which clearly explained where they came from, and the place of their marriage.

Finding they had no clear idea as to what an *Americano* might be, I tried to explain by saying that we were descendants of Christopher Columbus, but although in most towns there is a street called by his name, they shook their heads with no idea at all who *Cristobal Colon* might be.

In the morning it cleared off bright and warm, and we walked down to the village, and found how extremely fortunate we were. Four other diligences besides ours had arrived the previous afternoon, containing in all about an hundred persons, men, women and children. A few tried the village inn, but returned to the diligence instead, and there sat all night as uncomfortable as well could be imagined. At the road side, fires were blazing, and the hungry party, having procured something to eat, were engaged in cooking it. Looking at them, all wet, hungry, and bedraggled, we blefsed the power of the piece of gold. One stout, tall woman, with a little, insignificant husband, was particularly miserable, and poured forth volumes of bad French, while her lord stood meekly by, much like a bantam rooster well soaked with rain.

Strolling down to the stream, we found it a river half a mile in width, rushing furiously along, carrying away fences, crops, and trees. Small hopes of crofsing that day—so we walked up to the village, and congratulated ourselves that we were not compelled to stay in such a wretched, ill-favored, dirty place. The sun was warm, and we pafsed the morning in walking. About noon the water had decreased considerably, and by four o'clock a rope ferry

Chapter XIV.—Leaving Spain.

had been organized, sufficient to convey paſsengers and baggage. So bidding good-bye to our kind host and hoteſs, and leaving a substantial testimonial in her hand, we set forward again. Arriving on the other side, we took in exchange the diligence which had been detained there on the southward route, and proceeded on our way.

The ride over the Pyrenees is a very fine one, and the full moon, silvering the tops of the mountains and deepening the shadows of the valleys, perhaps rather heightened the effect.

In the middle of the night we reached the French frontier, and were compelled to dismount while the baggage was being searched. Accordingly about twenty sleepy people gathered in a small room, while all the baggage was unloaded and ranged upon the counter. Getting my pieces together, I called the attention of the official, and answering the familiar, "*Quelque chose à déclarer, Monsieur,*" in the negative, had my trunks marked without opening them.

The little man and his big wife were in a great stew. They were moving into France, and had all their worldly goods with them in trunks and boxes, and bundles, carefully corded up. Very minute inquiries were made concerning the contents of so much *impedimenta*, and suggestions of the necefsity of cutting the cords for the purpose of examination, were thrown out, causing the little man to turn pale with fright, and the large woman to grow scarlet with indignation. At last, after much talking—and perhaps the exchange of a few pesetas—*quien sabe?*—the packages were all marked, and with relieved minds the owners climbed into the stage again. About three o'clock we arrived at Perpignan, and were at last fairly out of Spain.

Chapter XV.—*General Remarks.*

SPAIN, as regards climate, is divided into three sections, running from east to west. The northern, with its rivers fed by the snows of the Pyrenées, is better irrigated than the rest of the country, but has cold winters and wet springs. The middle section is generally composed of vast and elevated plateaux of a mean elevation of about 1,900 feet, bounded and traversed by mountain ridges, which, however, are destitute of trees, and in consequence the country is dry. In winter the winds sweep unobstructed over the land, rendering it very cold, and in summer every thing is parched and withered by the blazing sun. The southern section, lower and sheltered by the mountains on the north, is more tropical in its temperature, with winters rather rainy than cold, hot summers, and delicious autumns and springs.

The mountains are rich in minerals and metals, and the products of the temperate and tropical zones may be cultivated in profusion.

The want of trees is a serious injury to the country. Mr. Marsh, in his "Man and Nature," says: "The laws of almost every European State more or lefs adequately secure the permanence of the forest; and I believe Spain is almost the only European land which has not made some public provision for the protection and restoration of the woods—the only country whose people systematically war upon the garden of God."

In a note he adds: "Antonio Ponz says: 'Nor would this be so great an evil, were not some of them declaimers against *trees*, thereby proclaiming themselves, in some sort, enemies of the works of God, who

Chapter XV.—General Remarks.

gave us the leafy abode of Paradise to dwell in, where we should be even now sojourning, but for the first sin which expelled us from it.'

"I do not know at what period the two Castiles were bared of their woods, but the Spaniard's proverbial 'hatred of a tree' is of long standing. Herrera vigorously combats this foolish prejudice; and Ponz, in the prologue to the ninth volume of his "Journey," says that many carried it so far as wantonly to destroy the shade and ornamental trees planted by the municipal authorities. 'Trees,' they contended, and still believe, 'breed birds, and birds eat up the grain.' Our author argues against the supposition of the 'breeding of birds by trees,' which, he says, is as absurd as to believe that an elm tree can yield pears; and he charitably suggests that the exprefsion is, perhaps, a *manière de dire*—a popular phrase, signifying simply that trees harbor birds."

Madrid is the great railroad centre of Spain. Thence ifsues one road north-west to

Bayonne, one north-east through Saragofsa to Barcelona, one south-easterly to Valencia, one southerly to Toledo, Cordova, Seville and Cadiz, and one westerly to Lisbon.

From a recent letter of W. C. Bryant, I extract the following:

"When I was in Spain, nine years since, there were but two good macadamized highways in the kingdom, of any considerable length, and these traversed it from north to south, connecting some of the principal cities. There were a few other carriage roads, scandalously neglected, and pafsable with difficulty, like that from Madrid to Alicante, or that between Alicante and Carthagena; but in general the realm was only intersected by bridle paths, along which the products of the country were conveyed to market on the backs of donkeys and mules. Nine years since there was only a bridle path to connect the two capitals of Spain and Portugal, and travelers went from Madrid to Lisbon on horseback — a curious illustration of the little intercourse between the two nations.

Chapter XV.—General Remarks.

Now you step into a railway carriage at Madrid, in the centre of the Peninsula, and in a few hours are at Lisbon, on the Atlantic. Railway lines now connect Spain with France, and form channels of communication between each province and the capital, and between each of them and the rest. The great line which takes the traveler southward from Madrid to Cordova, is one of the grandest enterprises of its kind. Ascending the Sierra Morena by a track winding along its northern slopes, it threads the grim defiles of that mountain range, between lofty precipices, crofses fearful chasms, pierces the ridges with frequent tunnels, spans torrent after torrent with iron bridges, runs in galleries hewn in the living rock, or between walls of masonry built to uphold the sliding soil, pafses along high and solid causeways, and descends into Andalusia by extensive sweeps on the mountain sides, overlooking the fertile valleys below. At every step it gives tokens of the vast expense at which it was constructed.

"But those who build railways expect to derive a profit from them, and those of Spain, with an inconsiderable exception or two, are a constant lofs to the proprietors. How could it well be otherwise? Here is a country which has so little commerce between its different districts, that it has not found it expedient to connect them by highways—and how can it be expected that its internal commerce will support an expensive system of railroads?

"I heard two Spanish gentlemen discufsing this subject the other day. One of them was saying that there was not trade enough to make the railways profitable, although the number of pafsengers was considerable. "Yes," said the other, "but trade will choose the cheapest methods of conveyance. The donkey's back is the old Spanish way of sending goods from place to place, and will continue to be used till we get something cheaper. The railway must underbid the donkey before it will be accepted as a substitute." He then went on to complain that goods sent by rail did

Chapter XV.—General Remarks.

not always reach their destination. One man had sent a number of skins of oil, and only a part of them came to hand. Another had put a different commodity on board of the train, with the same bad luck.

"The truth is, that the whole management of the Spanish railways is miserably slipshod, and deficient in order and punctuality. Long delays occur at the stopping places; petty accidents are always taking place; a train which should connect with another arrives too late, and the traveler finds himself obl'ged to wait twenty-four hours before he can proceed. It would not be at all strange if goods entrusted to such negligent hands should sometimes mifs their way.

"When, however, caution occasions delay, the Spanish railways are managed cautiously enough. The trains proceed slowly over bridges and along hillsides; they begin to slacken the speed of the engines for two or three miles before the train stops, so as to come to a pause in the most gradual manner pofsible. In pafsing the Sierra

Morena, we came to where a torrent had carried away one of the bridges, and a temporary support of the rails had been substituted. The train stopped, and we were detained an hour while this support was further strengthened. A French engineer connected with the road was on the train, and went out to see what was going on. When he returned he told us that there would not have been the least danger in pafsing the stream without a moment's delay, but that the conductor had refused to take the responsibility.

"The fares paid by pafsengers are high, and so, I hear, are the rates of freight; but that does not help the matter. There are interruptions in some of the railway lines, which, in consequence of their unproductivenefs, will probably remain as they are for some time to come. One of these we meet in crofsing the Pyrenées between Perpignan and Gerona; another is between Tarragona and Valencia. A railway has been completed leading from one of the main routes to Granada, but there is no train running upon it, and nobody knows when there will be. Spain, in short, is earlier with her railways than with her commerce, and the donkey still maintains a succefsful rivalry with the locomotive. Her railways are much like her rivers—channels for a current to flow in, but the current bears no proportion to the spaciousnefs of the channel."

One of the chief influences of the railroads in Spain will be the introduction of new and liberal ideas, for it is a fact that railways, facilitating commerce and travel, constitute a moral power which no religious or secular opprefsion can, in the end, succefsfully withstand.

Of late, her manufactures and commerce have largely increased, and education, though at a shamefully low ebb, has begun to revive. The confiscation of large church revenues afforded means for attracting foreign enterprise, and when the last of the Bourbons shall have disappeared, her advance bids fair to be rapid.

It is curious to examine the laws of Spain

in force only sixty or seventy years ago, in estimating the progrefs of the nation. I cite a few from a work published in 1805, and translated by an English barrister in 1825:

"Natural born subjects are prohibited, under pain of lofs of property and perpetual banishment, from going out of the kingdom for the purpose of study, excepting in the universities of Bologna, Coimbra, Rome, and Naples."

"They can not wear other clothes than those manufactured in the kingdom."

It was prohibited to grant the rights of naturalization to foreigners, who were only permitted to use the clothes they brought, contrary to the ordinance, for the space of six months after they entered Spain.

"It may be added that amongst us the following, and other like punishments, being considered barbarous, are obsolete: Burning alive, *unlefs for being a Jew,*" etc., etc.

"Advocates who do not practice or pursue their profefsion according to law, or are

Chapter XV.—General Remarks.

guilty of falsehood and malice, pay all the damages and prejudices they may cause to the parties, *besides double the amount.*" This might be advantageously re-enacted in most cities of the present day.

Blasphemers were of two kinds. The first of God and the most holy Virgin (*Maria Santifsima*). These had their tongues cut out and received one hundred stripes, if the crime were committed in court, and if out of it, had half their property confiscated, instead of receiving the stripes. The second clafs—blasphemers of the king—had half their property confiscated if they had children, and all if they had none, besides suffering ten years' condemnation to the galleys. This rule might seriously affect Mr. Ashley and General Butler, if it were in force in our country at present.

These laws, however, are not severe enough for the present Government of Spain, as the Governor of Castile has lately ifsued a proclamation that all persons who write, edit, or print papers against religion, the Queen, or the Government, shall be punished with death! From writing, the progrefs to speaking will be easy, and the subjects of Queen Isabella will have as great religious, but not as great civil liberty, as those of Philip II.

The sender of a challenge forfeited his property, and fighting a duel was punished with lofs of property and life. The receiver of a challenge was punished with banishment.

For being excommunicated thirty days, a man was fined six hundred maravedis; if he should remain so six months, he must pay six thousand maravedis; after that he was fined one hundred per day, and banished from the place, under pain, in case of returning, of confiscation of his property. So that a party who paid his two dollars, and was excommunicated for speaking to a woman in the Cathedral at Granada, stood a chance of paying dear for his thoughtlefsnefs.

Heretics could neither inherit nor be witnefses, and were liable to be punished with confiscation of property. They were

Chapter XV.—General Remarks.

pronounced heretics by the Inquisition, but the penalty was inflicted by the civil tribunals.

Playing at cards, or dice, in public, was forbidden, unlefs something to eat immediately was played for.

Beggars who could work might be driven out of the place, and receive fifty stripes.

The following may be commended to the various clerical and lay patrons of lotteries:

"Raffles and games of chance, *even under pretense of devotion*, are prohibited under the penalty of forfeiture of the things raffled for; and, besides, the price put down or paid to raffle, with as much more on the part of those who put it down or pay it."

Just now, it would be difficult to state whether any law except the will of the Queen and her advisers will be observed. Having laid aside the constitution, banished her husband and sister, and various prominent Liberals, and entrusted herself to the guidance of the absolutists in Church and

State, those who hope for the future welfare of Spain can only trust to the moral certainty that a re-action must result sooner or later.

The traveler in Spain, as in other countries, must expect to put up with many inconveniences. He must not get into an ill humor if the cars be slow, or the diligences meet with disaster; if men insist upon closing windows, while they smoke, through the night, in a confined space, or puff cigarettes between the courses at breakfast; or, in small towns, sit with their hats on at meals; if the waitrefs at a hotel is crofs, and leads him about from one uncomfortable room to another, without showing him the best for a time, when he arrives at a town at a late hour, he must forgive her; if the beggars pester him, he must be ready to smile, and if not willing, or prepared, to scatter coppers, to say, "God go with you;" he must submit with good grace to the extortion of paying three or four dollars for a lunch of a chicken and a few sandwiches, or three or four per cent. for exchange on London, payable in paper, which he must afterwards exchange for gold at a lofs of two or three per cent.; he must forego the luxury of fires, and of good tea and coffee, contenting himself with a brazier and excellent chocolate; he must be willing, with Sterne, to spend a shilling or two, more or lefs, without being made unhappy thereby, just as if he were riding in a hack, in one of our American cities; in a word, he must be prepared to encounter either evil or good fortune in the spirit of a true traveling philosopher.

So doing, shall he reap great pleasure and profit from his labor of travel.

www.ingramcontent.com/pod-product-compliance
Lightning Source LLC
Chambersburg PA
CBHW030256170426
43202CB00009B/759